UnHide Yourself

Break Free
From
Bias, Stigma &
Stereotypes

Empower Yourself
Empower Your Team

Maria Nathalia M. Drueco

Published by MariaNatha Press
Published in Canada.

Limit of Liability/Disclaimer of Warranty:
Neither the publisher nor the author is engaged in rendering legal or other professional services through this book. If expert assistance is required, the services of appropriate professionals should be sought. The publisher and the author shall have neither liability nor responsibility to any person or entity with respect to any loss or damage caused directly or indirectly by the information in this publication.

ISBN: 9798853292055

Title: UnHide Yourself is a pending trademark

To order more copies for you or your team, please visit www.theinclusionjourney.com

DEDICATION

To Almighty God, Who makes all things possible.

To my husband, Jayson, the wind beneath my wings.

To my children, Josh, Jared & Jerica, my inspirations.

*To my parents, Luz and Dilbert, and siblings, Shylle & Ann,
my support system.*

To all breaking free from bias, stigma, and stereotypes.

To all fostering an inclusive, equitable society.

With love and hope,

Maria Nathalia M. Drueco

Contents

PREFACE

Welcome to **UnHide Yourself™: Break Free from Bias, Stigma, and Stereotypes.**

This book is a heartfelt journey that aims to empower individuals like you to rise above the limitations imposed by bias, stigma, and stereotypes. Before we dive into the heart of the book, I want to share some thoughts and set the stage for what you can expect.

First and foremost, this book will not be a comprehensive guidebook on definitions and terms related to diversity, equity, and inclusion. There are already numerous resources available that provide in-depth explanations of these concepts. Instead, **UnHide Yourself™: Break Free from Bias, Stigma, and Stereotypes** provides a unique perspective and approach to addressing bias, stigma and stereotypes and creating change.

What makes this book unique is that it draws upon my personal experiences as an immigrant, a woman of color, and a professional who has worked in the field of diversity, equity, and inclusion. It is a culmination of my journey, filled with stories, insights, and practical strategies that have shaped my understanding and fueled my passion for creating a more inclusive and equitable society.

UnHide Yourself ™ takes personal development to a higher level, empowering readers with actionable strategies to catalyze systemic change. It goes beyond merely focusing on individual growth and instead guides readers on how to become champions of inclusivity and challenge biases both within themselves and throughout their organizations.

The book will bring you to a transformative journey filled with real-life anecdotes, empowering lessons, and inspiring examples of individuals and organizations that have shattered stereotypes and championed inclusivity. From mindset and self-confidence to overcoming challenges and maintaining work-life balance, we delve into essential skills for personal and leadership development. By addressing unconscious bias, stigma, stereotypes, and microaggressions, we equip you with the tools to create a truly inclusive environment.

As you embark on this adventure, you will discover the power of allyship and learn how to advocate for systemic change. My aim is to inform, educate, and inspire you to take bold action, both for personal growth and empowering your team. By embracing the principles and practical actions within these pages, you'll be equipped to create meaningful change in your spheres of influence, transforming yourself and your organization into a beacon of inclusivity and progress.

This book is about more than just my story. It's about yours too. Whether you seek personal growth, strive to build an inclusive workplace, or want to make a positive impact, this book is for you. It's a call to action for all the dreamers and doers who want to break down barriers and create a world where everyone can shine. It's a reminder that your voice matters, your experiences are valid, and your contributions are essential in shaping a kinder and more compassionate society.

Buckle up, my friend. We're going on a journey of self-discovery, pushing boundaries, and celebrating wins along the way.

As we embark on this journey of breaking free from bias, stigma and stereotypes, this book goes beyond the written word. The book is not just meant to be read but also crafted as a topic designed for engaging speaking engagements, workshops and presentations. Beyond the pages, its content is intended to inspire discussions, spark meaningful conversations, and foster a deeper understanding of the transformative power of challenging bias, stigma, and stereotypes. If you're interested in exploring the possibilities of arranging a speaking engagement, workshop, or presentation, please reach out to Maria at maria@theinclusionjourney.com

I hope this book becomes your trusted companion, cheering you on as you embrace your uniqueness, challenge the norms, and create a world where diversity is celebrated. Let's break those biases, shatter those stereotypes, and create a future where everyone has a fair shot at success.

Terms of Use

Limited Use License:

By using the models, frameworks, blueprint, tools, and worksheets provided in this book, you are granted a limited, non-exclusive, and non-transferable license. This license allows you to use the provided materials solely within the context of the book for personal learning and non-commercial purposes.

Attribution:

When using or referencing the models, frameworks, blueprint, tools, and worksheets from this book, you must provide proper attribution. Proper attribution includes acknowledging the source as **UnHide Yourself™** *: **Break Free From Bias, Stigma and Stereotypes*** by Maria Nathalia Drueco of *The Inclusion Journey* and providing appropriate references where applicable.

No Warranty:

All models, frameworks, blueprint, tools, and worksheets provided in this book are provided "as is," without any warranties or guarantees of any kind. Maria Nathalia Drueco of The Inclusion Journey makes no representations or warranties regarding the accuracy, functionality, or fitness for a particular purpose of these materials.

Limitation of Liability:
Under no circumstances shall Maria Nathalia Drueco of The Inclusion Journey be liable for any direct, indirect, incidental, special, or consequential damages resulting from the use of the models, frameworks, blueprint, tools, and worksheets in this book.

Modification and Derivative Works:
Readers are not permitted to modify, adapt, or create derivative works based on the provided models, frameworks, blueprint, tools, and worksheets without the explicit written permission of Maria Nathalia Drueco of The Inclusion Journey.

Third-Party Components:
If this book includes any third-party models, frameworks, blueprint, tools, or worksheets,

Maria Nathalia Drueco of The Inclusion Journey has obtained the necessary permissions for their inclusion and distribution. Any third-party components will be appropriately attributed, and readers are expected to comply with the relevant licensing terms.

Updates and Revisions:
Maria Nathalia Drueco of The Inclusion Journey may update or revise the content, including the models, frameworks, blueprint, tools, and worksheets, from time to time. It is recommended that readers refer to the latest version available for the most up-to-date information.

Termination:
This license is effective until terminated. Maria Nathalia Drueco of The Inclusion Journey reserves the right to terminate this license at any time if you fail to comply with these terms of use. Upon termination, you must immediately cease the use of the provided models, frameworks, blueprint, tools, and worksheets.

Compliance with Laws:

Readers are expected to comply with all applicable laws and regulations when using the models, frameworks, blueprint, tools, and worksheets from this book.

By using any of the models, frameworks, blueprint, tools, and worksheets provided in this book, you agree to be bound by these terms of use. If you do not agree with these terms, you must not use the provided materials.

For any questions or requests related to these terms of use, please contact Maria Nathalia Drueco by email: maria@theinclusionjourney.com

Maria Nathalia Drueco
The Inclusion Journey
2023

Disclaimer

While this book aims to empower individuals to reclaim their voices and embrace their true potential, it is important to note that the work of breaking down biases, stereotypes, and stigmas is not solely the responsibility of those who have experienced them. Achieving personal empowerment is just one part of the equation towards creating an equitable and inclusive world. The collective responsibility to dismantle these barriers lies with individuals of all backgrounds, irrespective of skin color, ethnicity, gender, or ability. It is through collective action, allyship, and a commitment to challenging systemic injustices that we can work towards a more inclusive and equitable society for all.

Author's Note

In this book, it is important to note that the experiences and stories shared are based on real-life events and personal reflections. However, the intention is not to generalize or speak on behalf of all individuals who have faced similar challenges. Each person's journey is unique, and while the narratives presented here aim to shed light on common themes and experiences, they may not fully capture the breadth of diverse experiences within marginalized communities. It is essential to approach these stories with empathy and an understanding that they represent a snapshot of individual experiences.

This book is a memoir, and the mention of some companies is for historical accuracy and personal recollection only. There is no intention to harm or damage the companies' reputation. Additionally, to protect the privacy and confidentiality of individuals and organizations, some names have been changed or pseudonyms have been used throughout the book. This decision was made to create a safe and respectful environment for sharing personal stories while ensuring the anonymity and privacy of those involved.

> The color of my skin,
> the cadence of my speech,
> the tapestry of my race and
> the aspect of my gender
> do not define the depths of
> my abilities.

Maria Drueco

INTRODUCTION

In the intricate fabric of today's organizations and society, the systems we have in place were not inherently designed to accommodate the diverse experiences of people of color, immigrants, and other marginalized groups. The journey towards a truly inclusive and equitable world is ongoing, marked by the need to confront biases, stigma, and stereotypes that continue to affect the lives of individuals from underrepresented communities. It is within this complex landscape that the story of **UnHide Yourself™: Break Free from Bias, Stigma & Stereotypes** unfolds.

As the author of this deeply personal account, I share my journey toward empowerment as a woman of color and immigrant in Canada.

In 2007, I made the life-altering decision to leave my home country, the Philippines, with my husband and three young children. My husband and I had great jobs, our two boys went to a private school, and we could travel to some parts of the country and even outside the country. We lived a privileged life back home.

"Why immigrate?" is a question I've encountered numerous times.

Fueled by the profound desire to create a better future for our children, we made a life-changing decision. We knew that in our home country, opportunities were limited, and we wanted to offer our children the chance to explore boundless possibilities and reach their full potential. It meant leaving behind a life of privilege and comfort. Still, the prospect of providing our children with a brighter and more promising future was the ultimate driving force behind our decision.

My husband and I embarked on a courageous journey, ready to start anew, knowing that we would have to build our careers from the ground up once again. We understood that the positions we held in our previous jobs might not be immediately attainable, and we were prepared to explore different industries to find opportunities to grow and thrive.

However, I was not ready for the challenge and the limitations placed upon us by stereotypes and cultural norms.

Arriving in Canada, I found myself navigating a landscape filled with judgment based on the color of my skin, the way I spoke, and the traditions I held dear. These biases threatened to overshadow my dreams, but I was determined to rise above them. My career aspirations led me to defy expectations and succeed in fields traditionally dominated by men, setting up my own business and shifting careers until I was at the place where I loved the work I was doing, proving that my capabilities were not limited by societal stereotypes.

Through education, self-reflection, and personal growth, I learned to value my worth and find the courage to unapologetically be myself. I became aware of the transformative power of embracing my unique experiences and perspectives, breaking free from the limitations imposed by others.

UnHide Yourself™: Break Free from Bias, Stigma and Stereotypes is a culmination of my personal and professional journey, infused with a passion for driving positive change. The book draws from my extensive experience in diversity, equity, and inclusion (DEI), talent management, intercultural training, and antiracism work. The insights I have gained through my work in DEI have given me a unique perspective on the challenges faced by individuals from marginalized groups and a deeper understanding of the systemic barriers within organizations and society. I have witnessed firsthand the transformative power of implementing inclusive practices and creating environments where everyone can thrive.

In this book, I use the term "marginalized groups" to encompass a wide range of social communities facing various challenges, including BIPOC (Black, Indigenous, and People of Color), immigrants, people with disabilities, 2SLGBTQI+ individuals, and others who are often underrepresented in various aspects of society. It's important to acknowledge that many of these marginalized groups are also disproportionately underrepresented in certain spaces and sectors.

Within the pages of this book lies the promise of empowerment for those who are marginalized, immigrants seeking their place in a foreign land, women striving to shatter glass ceilings, people with disabilities and who are stigmatized, those who identify as 2SLGBTQI+ and those who identify themselves as Persons of Color, navigating a landscape riddled with systemic challenges. It offers stories of resilience, courage, and triumph, providing inspiration and guidance to overcome obstacles and embrace their unique identities.

UnHide Yourself™: Break Free from Bias, Stigma and Stereotypes is a powerful guide for those facing challenges and barriers. It offers practical strategies, helpful guidance, and strong support to overcome obstacles and boost confidence. It's like a compass that helps you find your way through tough times and believe in yourself. The promise is simple yet profound—unlock the potential within you and navigate courageous conversations, even in the most daunting and unsafe spaces.

And lastly, **UnHide Yourself™: Break Free from Bias, Stigma and Stereotypes** serves as a beacon of inspiration for those who aim to be allies and advocates of positive change. Whether you're just starting your journey or looking to enhance your allyship skills, this book equips you with practical tools, empathy, and the resolve to contribute to positive change. This book will help you gain insights into the challenges faced by immigrants, women, and BIPOC individuals, empowering them to actively participate in creating equitable and diverse environments. Embrace the opportunity to stand alongside those whose experiences may differ from yours. You can help cultivate an ecosystem where every voice is heard and valued, and everyone can thrive unapologetically.

Chapter 1
Unveiling Bias, Stigma, Stereotypes and
Their Impact on Marginalized groups

"Unveiling bias is unlocking the world of possibilities; as the blinders fall away, the vast landscape of human potential comes into clear view."
- *Maria N. Drueco*

Bias, stigma, and stereotypes are multifaceted constructs that profoundly affect our perceptions, interactions, and opportunities. To ensure we share the same understanding of what these constructs are and how they are different, let's define the terms:

Bias encompasses our preconceived attitudes and beliefs about individuals or groups based on certain characteristics. It's the tendency to hold favorable or unfavorable attitudes, beliefs, or judgments about individuals or groups based on certain characteristics such as race, gender, age, religion, sexual orientation, or disability. Biases can be conscious or unconscious, influencing how we perceive and interact with others, leading to unfair treatment or favoritism.

Stigma is a negative stereotype or label that society assigns to certain individuals or groups based on perceived characteristics deviating from societal norms. Stigmatized individuals often face social exclusion, discrimination, and reduced opportunities due to the negative assumptions and judgments attached to them.

Stereotypes are widely held beliefs and oversimplified generalizations about members of a particular group. These assumptions can be based on race, gender, ethnicity, religion, and other characteristics. Stereotypes can be harmful, perpetuating biased views and limiting the potential of individuals by reducing them to a set of predetermined traits.

To contextualize these constructs, let's go through some scenarios typically experienced by women and people of color in the workplace.

Bias Against an Immigrant Woman of Color
Karen, a highly qualified woman of color and immigrant, is applying for a senior management position in a renowned organization. Karen possesses exceptional skills, extensive experience, and a track record of impressive achievements in her field. Despite her qualifications, she notices subtle signs of bias during the interview process.

As Karen discusses her accomplishments, she observes that her qualifications are questioned more rigorously than those of other candidates. The interviewers seem skeptical about her ability to fit into the company culture due to her cultural background and accent. Karen also encounters microaggressions disguised as innocent inquiries about her personal life and commitments, implying that her commitment to the job may be questionable.

Karen was not offered the position despite her best efforts to showcase her skills and abilities. Instead, the role is given to a candidate from a more dominant cultural background, who may have a different level of expertise or experience than Karen.

In this example, Karen faces bias against her as a woman of color and an immigrant. The interviewers' preconceived attitudes and beliefs about her cultural background and accent influenced their perception of her qualifications and potential fit within the organization. This bias leads to unequal treatment, hindering Karen's chances of securing the position, even though she is highly qualified for the role.

Such instances of bias can profoundly impact the professional advancement of women of color and immigrants, perpetuating systemic barriers that limit their opportunities for career growth and development. Addressing and dismantling such biases is crucial to creating a more inclusive and equitable workplace where everyone can thrive based on their skills, qualifications, and contributions, regardless of their background or identity.

Stigmas Faced by an Immigrant Woman of Color

Let's consider the experience of Aisha, a highly skilled woman of color who moved to a new country to pursue better career opportunities. Aisha's expertise and qualifications are well-regarded in her home country. Still, upon arriving in the new country, she encounters various stigmas and stereotypes related to her immigrant status and cultural background.

- *Cultural Stereotypes*: Aisha faces stereotypes and assumptions about her cultural norms and practices. For instance, some colleagues may assume that she holds traditional views or lacks fluency in the local language based on her ethnicity. This stigma may lead to her being treated as an outsider or limited to certain roles in the workplace.
- *Negative Perceptions:* Aisha may experience negative perceptions based on the country she comes from. Some may assume that her educational background or work experience is inferior, leading to underestimating her skills and capabilities.

Along with these stigmas come their consequences:

- **Imposter Syndrome:** Due to the stigma attached to being an immigrant woman of color, Aisha may develop imposter syndrome, feeling like she doesn't belong or isn't qualified for her position. This self-doubt can impact her confidence and hinder her professional growth.

- **Lack of Cultural Understanding:** Aisha may face challenges finding common ground with colleagues who are less familiar with her cultural background. This lack of understanding may lead to misunderstandings or misinterpretations of her actions and communication style.

- **Isolation and Exclusion:** Due to stigmatization, Aisha may feel isolated and excluded from certain social circles or networking opportunities within the workplace. This lack of inclusion can hinder her professional networking and career advancement.

- **Tokenism:** In some instances, Aisha may be tokenized and seen as a diversity checkbox rather than recognized for her unique skills and contributions. This tokenism can diminish her sense of belonging and value within the organization.

- **Limited Leadership Opportunities:** The stigma attached to her identity as a woman of color immigrant may lead to limited access to leadership and advancement opportunities. Despite her qualifications, Aisha may face barriers in accessing roles with higher responsibilities and decision-making authority.

These examples illustrate the stigmas and their impact on women of color who are also immigrants in the workplace.

It's a Vicious Cycle!
Bias, stereotypes, stigma, and discrimination are interconnected and often reinforce each other, creating a vicious cycle that perpetuates inequality, inequity, injustice and marginalization. These constructs coexist and feed into one another, amplifying their impact on individuals and communities. Understanding this complex interplay is crucial in addressing systemic issues and promoting inclusivity.

Let's go back to how we understand these constructs:

Bias and Stereotypes: Bias refers to the preconceived attitudes and beliefs we hold about individuals or groups based on their characteristics, such as race, gender, or ethnicity. Stereotypes are fixed, oversimplified generalizations that are often based on these biases. When biased attitudes influence our perceptions, we are more likely to accept and reinforce stereotypes, which inform our behavior and decision-making.

Stereotypes and Stigma: Stereotypes can create stigmas, which are negative labels or assumptions attached to certain individuals or groups. Stigmas are born out of stereotypes and are used to categorize people based on perceived differences or characteristics. Stigmas further isolate and marginalize individuals, affecting their self-esteem and social and economic advancement opportunities.

Stigma and Discrimination: Stigma can manifest in discriminatory behaviors and practices, as individuals or institutions act upon the negative labels and assumptions they hold. Discrimination can occur in various settings, such as the workplace, education, healthcare, justice system and social interactions. Discrimination reinforces the stigmatization process, creating a cycle that hinders progress and perpetuates inequality, injustice and inequity.

Discrimination and Bias: Experiencing discrimination can strengthen and reinforce existing biases. When individuals face discrimination, it may confirm their preconceived notions about certain groups, leading to a self-fulfilling prophecy. This can further fuel biased attitudes and discriminatory behaviors, continuing the cycle of inequity..

Are you feeling a bit puzzled?

Let's look at Figure 1: The Vicious Cycle

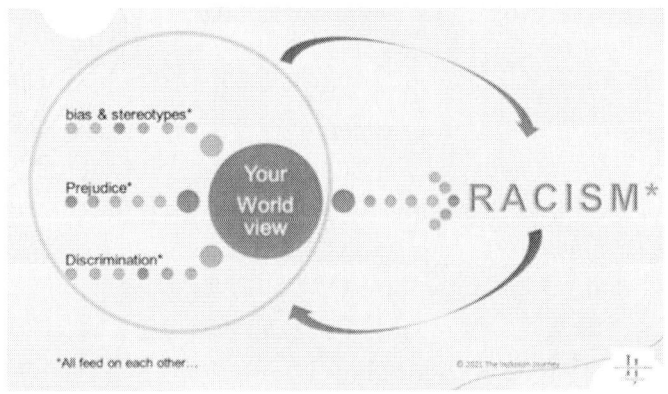

Figure 1: **The Vicious Cycle**

Figure 1 shows how bias, stigma, stereotypes, prejudice and discrimination affect our world view and perpetuates racism and societal inequity. Prejudice is a preconceived opinion or judgment, bias is an inclination or favoritism, stigma is a negative perception toward certain characteristics, stereotype is a fixed belief about a group, and discrimination is unfair treatment based on characteristics or perceived attributes. All these concepts are interconnected. All feed on each other. Overcoming and addressing these issues are crucial steps toward fostering a more inclusive and equitable society.

The Chain of Inequity

Since these are heavy concepts, I like to use metaphors when explaining these to my workshop participants.

- Prejudice is like a foggy lens that distorts our view, blurring the truth behind hazy judgments.
- Bias is the invisible scale that tilts our perceptions, tipping the balance in favor of one side while leaving others in the shadows.
- Stigma casts a long shadow, lurking behind like a relentless cloud that follows those it seeks to darken, marking them as outcasts and isolating them from full acceptance.
- Stereotypes are like rigid molds, shaping people into cookie-cutter forms, overlooking the beautiful tapestry of individuality.
- Discrimination builds walls, erecting barriers that hinder progress and limit the flowering potential of every human soul.

Each concept has unique characteristics and implications and can perpetuate and reinforce each other, forming a chain of adverse effects on individuals and society. Because they're interconnected and interdependent, I likened them to a "chain," the **"chain of inequity,"** since each attitude/ action lead to another. They work in unison to maintain unjust systems and behaviors. It's a powerful way to summarize the negative impact of these concepts on individuals and society.

It's essential to recognize that bias, stereotypes, stigma, prejudice and discrimination deeply influence our beliefs, behaviors, and actions. This underscores the critical need for a comprehensive, intersectional, and systemic approach to tackle these issues effectively. By addressing them at their root and considering the complexities of how they intertwine, we can create lasting change and foster a more inclusive and equitable world.

Chapter 2
Understanding the Impact of Discrimination and Microaggression

"Seeing others through a clear lens of openness and acceptance, we uncover a mosaic of shared experiences that connects us all as fellow travelers on the journey of life."
- *Maria N. Drueco*

I never imagined that I would find myself back in the pharmaceutical field again. After spending more than 11 years working with Pfizer, I thought that chapter of my career was closed. However, my experience in different areas with a leading medical laboratory service provider in Alberta made me realize that laboratory work wasn't fulfilling my professional aspirations. I missed the challenge and high-pressure environment that came with pharmaceutical sales.

When I stumbled upon a job opportunity as a pharmaceutical representative for Takeda Canada, which was launching two major products in the country, I knew I had to go for it.

The position offered me the chance to cover a third of the province of Alberta as my territory.

I updated my resume and applied, hoping for a fresh start in a familiar industry.

During my early days in this new role, I encountered an incident that shed light on the subtle racial bias I faced as an immigrant. It occurred while waiting for my turn to do a product presentation at a doctor's office. As I stepped into the doctor's clinic for the first time, I was eager and well-prepared to present the benefits of the medication I represented. However, I couldn't shake the feeling that the receptionist's demeanor toward me had changed noticeably. It left me wondering what caused the shift in her attitude.

While she engaged in friendly conversations with other representatives, her attitude towards me turned dismissive. She was clearly uninterested in engaging with me and treated me differently compared to other pharmaceutical reps, all of whom happened to be White. I couldn't help but wonder if my ethnicity played a role in her behavior.

As minutes turned into what felt like an eternity, I noticed other representatives who arrived after me being called in before me. Doubt started to creep in, making me question whether my professional abilities were being judged based on factors beyond my control. I brushed off the incident, telling myself it was a one-off experience, and that the receptionist needed more time to warm up to me.

However, as time passed and I continued working in this role for two years, the receptionist's attitude toward me remained the same. She never warmed up to me, and I still felt a sense of distance and coldness whenever I visited that doctor's office.

In moments like these, I truly realized the impact of the subtle racial bias I faced as an immigrant. It left me feeling isolated and undermined as if my presence and expertise were deemed less important simply because of my cultural background. This experience opened my eyes to the challenges individuals from underrepresented communities face.

The Psychological and Emotional Toll

Discrimination, fueled by bias, stigma, and stereotypes, exacts a heavy toll on our psychological and emotional well-being. I can vividly recall the moments when I encountered such bias at my workplace, and the aftermath was profound. The hurt I experienced ran deep, and it led me to question my own worth, wondering why I was subjected to such treatment.

Research affirms the impact of such experiences, showing that individuals who face discrimination often suffer from decreased self-esteem, increased levels of stress and anxiety, and even higher rates of depression and mental health disorders.

In Canada, these effects are strikingly evident. A study conducted by Statistics Canada revealed that racialized individuals experience higher levels of psychological distress than their non-racialized counterparts. Seeing the toll discrimination takes on mental well-being is disheartening, affecting individuals' ability to thrive and contribute fully to their personal and professional lives.

Barriers to Career Advancement

Throughout history, marginalized communities have faced numerous barriers to career advancement. These barriers perpetuate a significant wage gap, limited opportunities for promotion, and restricted access to leadership positions. I remember the struggles I encountered as an immigrant woman of color, facing biases that made it challenging to break through the glass ceiling and achieve the career growth I aspired to.

In Canada, studies by organizations like Catalyst have shed light on the challenges women face in reaching leadership positions, particularly women of color. Indigenous peoples and racialized individuals also confront barriers that hinder their career progression and limit their access to decision-making roles. These disparities highlight the urgent need to address systemic biases and create inclusive environments where everyone has an equal opportunity to succeed.

Unpacking Microaggressions

Microaggressions, subtle but harmful acts of discrimination, continue to plague our society. These insidious behaviors undermine a person's identity and perpetuate stereotypes, creating a hostile and exclusionary environment. I recall instances where seemingly innocent comments or gestures belittled my experiences as an immigrant, leaving me feeling marginalized and unheard.

The roots of microaggressions can be traced back to historical injustices and deeply embedded biases. Despite increased awareness, these behaviors persist. Studies have shown that individuals from marginalized communities experience microaggressions at alarming rates. According to research by the

Canadian Centre for Diversity and Inclusion, 80% of Indigenous peoples report experiencing microaggressions in the workplace.

Microaggressions manifest differently for individuals based on their unique intersectional identities, encompassing race, gender, sexual orientation, disability, and more. These intersecting aspects of our identity contribute to a complex web of experiences, shaping how microaggressions impact us on multiple levels.

For example, a person who identifies as a woman of color may face microaggressions from racial and gender biases. These microaggressions can be comments, gestures, or subtle actions that undermine her experiences, perpetuate stereotypes, and marginalize her within social and professional settings.

In another scenario, an individual who identifies as a member of the S2LGBTQI+ community may encounter microaggressions related to their sexual orientation or gender identity. These microaggressions can range from subtle slights to overt forms of discrimination, creating an environment that questions their authenticity, validity, and sense of belonging.

Understanding the nuanced nature of microaggressions helps us recognize how individuals experience these acts of discrimination. It underscores the importance of intersectionality in our conversations on inclusion. It prompts us to approach these issues with empathy, openness, and a commitment to dismantling systemic biases.

Harmful Effects of Microaggressions and Stereotypes

Impact on the Individual
In the study conducted by Sue et al. (2007), titled "Racial microaggressions in everyday life: Implications for clinical practice," the researchers shed light on the detrimental effects of microaggressions, particularly on mental health.

The study reveals that microaggressions can result in various harmful effects on an individual, including:

- *Psychological Distress:* Microaggressions elicit emotional responses such as anger, frustration, sadness, and anxiety, leading to psychological distress.
- *Impact on Self-Esteem:* Continuous exposure to microaggressions can erode an individual's self-esteem and self-worth, causing them to doubt their abilities and value.

- *Increased Stress:* Microaggressions contribute to heightened stress levels, which can negatively affect physical and mental health.
- *Alienation and Isolation:* Microaggressions create a sense of alienation and isolation, making individuals feel marginalized and excluded from their social or professional environments.
- *Cumulative Effect:* The cumulative impact of repeated microaggressions can have long-term implications for an individual's mental well-being.

These stories and statistics serve as reminders of the urgent need to address discrimination and promote inclusivity. By understanding the psychological toll, the barriers to career advancement, and the prevalence of microaggressions, we recognize the importance of courageous conversations in effecting change.

You might wonder if these experiences are isolated incidents or if they reflect larger systemic issues. The truth is that discrimination, biases, and barriers to success are pervasive in our society. By acknowledging this reality, we can move towards addressing these issues and creating environments that promote equality and respect.

One common mistake is dismissing or downplaying the experiences of those who face microaggression or discrimination. It is crucial to approach these stories with an open mind, acknowledging the validity of these experiences and using them as a catalyst for change. Another mistake is assuming that microaggression and discrimination is solely an individual issue. It is important to recognize the systemic nature of discrimination and work towards dismantling the structures that perpetuate inequality.

During my early career, I faced various instances of subtle bias and microaggressions. These experiences left me feeling diminished and questioning my abilities. However, through self-reflection and the support of mentors, I gained the courage to overcome these obstacles and navigate the complexities of a biased work environment. In a later chapter, we will dive deep into ways on how to respond to microaggression, stereotypes and discrimination.

Impact on the Team

When it comes to the impact of microaggressions and stereotypes on the team, it is important to recognize that these harmful behaviors have significant consequences for team dynamics and collaboration. The study conducted by Richards and Hackett (2012) sheds light on the implications of cultural diversity in teams and provides insights into the challenges that arise from microaggressions and stereotypes.

Here are some of the key impacts of microaggressions and stereotypes on the team:

1. **Reduced Psychological Safety:** Microaggressions and stereotypes create an environment where team members may not feel safe expressing their ideas or be their authentic selves. This lack of psychological safety hinders open communication, collaboration, and the sharing of diverse perspectives.

2. **Decreased Trust and Cohesion:** Microaggressions erode trust among team members, as they create feelings of disrespect and exclusion. Stereotypes perpetuate biases and preconceived notions, leading to divisions within the team and hindering cohesive teamwork.

3. **Impaired Creativity and Innovation:** When team members experience microaggressions or stereotypes, their confidence and willingness to contribute may be diminished. This stifles creativity and innovation, as individuals may hesitate to share their unique insights and ideas.

4. **Negative Impact on Decision-Making:** Microaggressions and stereotypes can

influence decision-making processes within the team. Biases and stereotypes may lead to unfair judgments and biased evaluations of team members' contributions, compromising the quality and fairness of decision-making.

5. ***Decreased Job Satisfaction and Engagement:*** Experiencing microaggressions and being subjected to stereotypes can significantly impact team members' job satisfaction and overall engagement. It creates a hostile work environment, contributing to feelings of dissatisfaction and demotivation.

Impact on the Organization

The impact of stereotypes and microaggressions on organizations is well-documented. Research suggests that these biases can have detrimental effects on organizational performance, employee well-being, and overall organizational culture. Here are some key impacts:

1. ***Decreased Employee Engagement:*** Stereotypes and microaggressions create a negative work environment that erodes employee engagement. When employees feel targeted or devalued based on their identity, their motivation and commitment to the organization may suffer, leading to decreased productivity and performance.

2.   *Increased Turnover and Attrition:* Persistent stereotypes and microaggressions can contribute to higher turnover rates and attrition among affected individuals. When employees face discrimination or are subject to biased treatment, they may seek employment opportunities elsewhere, resulting in talent loss and increased recruitment and training costs for the organization.

3.   *Impaired Collaboration and Innovation*: Stereotypes and microaggressions hinder effective collaboration and inhibit the free flow of ideas and creativity. When individuals feel marginalized or excluded due to biases, they may be less likely to contribute fully to team projects or share their unique perspectives. This can limit innovation and problem-solving capabilities within the organization.

4.   *Damaged Reputation and Employer Brand:* Organizations that allow stereotypes and microaggressions to persist may suffer reputational damage. Negative experiences and discriminatory practices can become known within industry or broader community, leading to a tarnished employer brand. This can impact the organization's ability to attract top talent and maintain positive relationships with stakeholders.

5.   *Legal and Financial Consequences:* Stereotypes and microaggressions can expose organizations to legal risks and financial

consequences. Discriminatory practices can result in legal complaints, lawsuits, and damage to the organization's reputation, leading to financial losses and potential legal penalties. Remember the lawsuits against Walmart, Tesla, Uber, and Google? These companies paid millions of dollars to settle discrimination cases filed by their employees.

Practical Actions

1. **Reflect:** Take a moment to reflect on your own experiences and biases. Consider how they may have shaped your perceptions of others and their opportunities for success.
2. **Educate:** Expand your knowledge about the experiences faced by marginalized communities. Engage with books, documentaries, and research studies to deepen your understanding of systemic issues and the impact of discrimination.
3. **Connect:** Engage in open and honest and respectful conversations with individuals from different backgrounds. Practice active listening and empathy to gain insights into their experiences and challenges they may face.
4. **Advocate:** Take action against discrimination. Speak up when you witness bias, microaggression or inequality in your personal and professional life. Support

initiatives and organizations that promote diversity, equity, and inclusion. Implement policies that address and prevent microaggressions and discrimination.

5. **Foster Inclusivity and create a psychologically safe environment:** Create an inclusive and respectful environment by actively seeking diverse perspectives and voices. Encourage collaboration and equal participation. Challenge stereotypes and promote fairness and respect in all interactions.

Change starts with individual actions. By taking these steps, you contribute to the collective effort of building inclusive environments and empowering positive change.

Chapter 3
The Power of Our Stories:
Sharing and Being Heard

When we embrace the power of our stories, we discover that being heard is not just about finding our voices but also lending an ear to the stories of others, igniting a profound transformation in how we relate to one another."
- Maria N. Drueco

Throughout my journey, I have discovered the transformative power of our stories and the importance of owning them. This chapter will explore how embracing vulnerability, breaking the silence, and overcoming fear and self-doubt can empower us to speak up, challenge discrimination, and foster inclusivity.

Embracing Vulnerability

Research has shown that embracing vulnerability creates stronger connections and fosters empathy. According to a study conducted by Brené Brown, a renowned researcher on vulnerability, individuals who embrace vulnerability have higher levels of self-worth and experience more authentic relationships (Brown, 2012). By allowing ourselves to be seen and heard authentically, despite the fear of judgment or rejection, we create spaces where genuine connections can flourish.

During a team-building workshop, we were encouraged to share personal stories of struggle and growth. As I listened to my colleagues open up about their challenges and fears, I felt a mix of apprehension and curiosity. Would I have the courage to share my own story?

As the room fell silent, I mustered up the courage to speak. I shared my experience of immigrating to a new country, leaving behind everything familiar, and facing numerous obstacles along the way. I talked about the doubts and insecurities I had to overcome and the resilience that kept me going. To my surprise, I saw nods of understanding and empathy.

At that moment, I realized the power of vulnerability. I created a space for others to connect and relate by sharing my authentic story. I learned that vulnerability is not a weakness but a strength that allows us to forge deeper connections and build genuine relationships.

Since that day, I have made a conscious effort to embrace vulnerability in both my personal and professional life. I've learned that opening myself up and allowing others to see the real me creates an atmosphere of trust and authenticity. Through vulnerability, I've built stronger connections and fostered empathy with those around me.

Reflecting on this journey of embracing vulnerability, I encourage you to do the same. Take the risk of being seen and heard, even if it feels uncomfortable. You never know how your story might resonate with someone else and inspire others to embrace their vulnerability. Let's create spaces where authenticity and connection thrive, and together, we can make a profound impact on ourselves and those around us.

Vulnerability as a Leader

Numerous research studies have shown that vulnerability is crucial in building trust within leadership. A study conducted by Harvard Business Review found that leaders who demonstrate vulnerability are more likely to establish trust with their teams (Gentry et al., 2017). When leaders are open and honest about their own challenges, insecurities, and mistakes, it creates an environment where team members feel safe to express themselves and take risks.

I experienced the power of vulnerability in leadership firsthand when I worked with a remarkable leader, Keith. He was known for his transparent and vulnerable leadership style. He openly shared his struggles, doubts, and lessons learned during team meetings. He would admit when he made mistakes and seek input from the team on how to improve.

This vulnerability created a sense of psychological safety within our team. We felt comfortable expressing our ideas, sharing our concerns, and seeking support. We knew our leader valued our opinions and was genuinely interested in our growth and success. Keith's vulnerability built trust and fostered a culture of innovation and collaboration.

One particular instance stands out in my mind. We were facing a critical project deadline, and the pressure was mounting. Instead of putting on a façade of unwavering confidence, Keith gathered the team and openly expressed his fears and uncertainties. He acknowledged our challenges and emphasized the importance of our collective effort. His vulnerability in that moment brought us closer together, instilling a sense of unity and shared responsibility.

Through this experience, I learned that vulnerability in leadership is not a sign of weakness but a strength that can inspire and motivate teams. It creates an environment where trust flourishes, enabling open communication, collaboration, and innovation. When leaders are willing to be vulnerable, it shows authenticity, and authenticity breeds trust.

As leaders, let us recognize the transformative power of vulnerability. We can foster a culture of trust, connection, and growth by embracing our vulnerability and creating a safe space for others to do the same. Let us lead with our hearts and minds open, inspiring our teams to reach new heights and achieve collective success.

Breaking the Silence: Why It Matters

Silence in the face of discrimination perpetuates the status quo and allows biases to persist. Research conducted by Harvard Business Review shows that organizations that foster an inclusive environment and encourage employees to speak up against discrimination and biases have higher levels of employee engagement and satisfaction (Harvard Business Review, 2019). By breaking the silence, we send a powerful message that discrimination will not be tolerated, leading to positive changes within our communities and workplaces.

Breaking the silence in the face of constant belittlement can be daunting. But there was a turning point in my journey when I finally mustered the courage to confront my supervisor. She had a pattern of picking on small things that non-white employees, especially Asian employees, did, seemingly to belittle us and undermine our confidence.

As days turned into weeks and months, I witnessed this recurring behavior towards myself and my fellow non-white colleagues. It became evident that our supervisor's actions were driven by biases and prejudices based on our racial backgrounds. Seeing her dismiss our contributions and consistently target us with condescending comments was disheartening.

The weight of her constant criticisms took a toll on my self-esteem and created a hostile work environment. I knew I couldn't let it continue without addressing the underlying issue of discrimination.

Summoning all my strength, I requested a meeting with my supervisor to discuss my concerns. Walking into her office, I carried the weight of the experiences shared by my colleagues who had faced similar mistreatment. Despite the risk of potential repercussions, I was resolute in my decision to speak up and address the issue head-on.

In a calm and composed tone, I addressed the issue directly, *"It seems that you perceive a pattern of consistently finding faults in what I do. Despite my confidence in knowing that the procedure is correct, it feels disheartening to continually face criticism for my work. Adding to the frustration, these criticisms often occur in front of my co-workers, which not only undermines my competency but also creates a sense of embarrassment and discomfort in the workplace. I think it's important for us to have a conversation about this behavior and how it is affecting me."*

There was a moment of silence as my supervisor absorbed my words. Her initial surprise turned into a defensive response, denying any biased treatment. However, armed with facts, I calmly presented evidence of the recurring mistreatment.

As the discussion unfolded, my supervisor's demeanor was consistent. She didn't offer an apology but instead insisted that she didn't mean to belittle me. In that moment, I realized the importance of highlighting the impact of our actions, regardless of intent. I calmly explained that while I understood her intentions may not have been malicious, the impact of her words and behavior had still created a negative and dismissive atmosphere.

In the following weeks and months, I noticed a significant shift in my supervisor's behavior towards me. She became more mindful of her words and actions, making a conscious effort to treat me with the respect and professionalism that I deserved. It was a small but meaningful shift that demonstrated her willingness to listen and learn from our conversation.

I believe that this positive change was not just limited to our interactions. I observed a shift in how she treated our non-white co-workers as well. She became more respectful to all, not just to our white co-workers. It was a testament to the power of speaking up and addressing issues of bias and discrimination in the workplace.

This experience taught me how to break the silence and address discrimination head-on. By confronting my supervisor, I stood up for myself, a reminder that our voices matter. Our voices have the power to drive change and foster a more inclusive and respectful workplace.

Indeed, if I had chosen to remain silent and not speak up about the mistreatment I experienced, the toxic behavior would have continued unchecked. Not only would it have perpetuated a harmful work environment, but the impact on my well-being would have been far worse. By finding the courage to address the issue, I advocated for myself and paved the way for positive change.

It is essential to recognize that remaining silent in the face of discrimination allows it to persist. By speaking up and shedding light on these issues, we challenge the status quo and create an opportunity for transformation. It may feel daunting and uncertain, especially when the fear of potential consequences lingers in the back of our minds. However, the cost of staying silent and enduring mistreatment far outweighs the temporary discomfort of speaking up.

Breaking the silence is a courageous step toward dismantling discriminatory practices. By shedding light on the issue, we create opportunities for change, promoting a workplace where everyone is valued and respected, regardless of race or ethnicity.

It is through our collective efforts and courageous conversations that we can dismantle harmful behaviors and create an environment where everyone feels valued and respected.

Overcoming Fear and Self-Doubt

Overcoming fear and self-doubt is a journey that allows us to tap into our true potential as advocates for change. Research has shown that resilience and self-belief are critical to overcoming these barriers.

A study published in the Journal of Positive Psychology found that individuals who cultivated self-compassion and practiced positive self-talk had higher levels of self-confidence and resilience (Neff & Germer, 2013). By gradually stepping out of our comfort zones and seeking support from allies and mentors, we can overcome fear and self-doubt and empower ourselves to make our voices heard.

I remember the exhilaration and nerves consumed me as I prepared for my first speaking engagement at a global conference for learning and development professionals. The opportunity to share my insights on effectively onboarding oneself in any role was a golden opportunity. Still, it also brought a wave of self-doubt and fear. Thoughts of inadequacy and questioning my expertise filled my mind, threatening to overshadow the significance of the moment.

Months before the event, I had sleepless nights that turned into moments of internal struggle as I battled my own insecurities. Fear threatened to overpower me, casting doubts on my ability to make a meaningful impact. In these moments of darkness, I realized the power of courage and the need to confront my self-imposed limitations.

Seeking support from family, trusted friends, and mentors became my lifeline. They reminded me of my strengths, the value of my experiences, and the unique perspective I could offer. With their encouragement, I began to challenge the negative self-talk and replace it with affirmations of self-belief.

I immersed myself in research and practice, preparing meticulously for the conference. Each moment of doubt became an opportunity for growth, pushing me to push beyond my comfort zone and embrace the vulnerability that comes with sharing personal stories and insights. Deep down, I knew I had something valuable to contribute, and I was determined to overcome my fears to make a difference.

Stepping onto the stage on the conference day, my heart raced with nervousness and excitement. But I refused to let fear dictate my actions. Taking a deep breath, I stood tall and spoke from the depths of my experiences with authenticity and vulnerability. The room was filled with eager faces, ready to engage in meaningful discussions.

To my delight, the audience responded positively. As one participant expressed, *'This has been the most practical session of the conference...they allowed me to express my pitfall and helped me work through it.'* Another attendee shared their appreciation, saying, *'Loved the concise tips and the introduction to higher-level concepts to run with.'* It was heartening to receive such specific feedback, knowing that my insights had been helpful and impactful.

At that moment, I realized the power of overcoming fear and self-doubt. By embracing my unique perspective, speaking my truth and sharing my knowledge, I empower myself and inspire others to do the same. The atmosphere of openness and shared understanding in the room reinforced the importance of expressing our insights and experiences, creating a ripple effect of empowerment and growth. Their positive response encouraged me to continue offering my knowledge and experience to empower others, fostering a community of growth and development.

That experience taught me a valuable lesson: fear and self-doubt may always linger, but they don't have to define our actions. It is the same when we are dealing with discriminatory behaviors. Unlocking our voice and challenging discrimination requires us to confront not only external barriers but also the internal obstacles that hold us back.

Examples of internal obstacles that can hinder us from speaking up and overcoming fear and challenging discrimination:

1. ***Self-doubt***: Feeling unsure about our abilities, knowledge, or expertise in a particular subject can create self-doubt. We may question whether our opinions or perspectives are valid, leading us to hesitate in sharing our thoughts.

2. ***Fear of judgment:*** The fear of being judged or criticized by others can be a significant internal obstacle. We worry about how our ideas or experiences will be received, fearing that we may face negative reactions or backlash.

3. ***Imposter syndrome***: Imposter syndrome refers to the persistent feeling of being a fraud, despite evidence of our accomplishments. We may doubt our competence and believe that we don't belong in certain spaces, which can

hinder us from speaking up and sharing our perspectives.

4. **Perfectionism**: Striving for perfection can create a fear of making mistakes or saying the wrong thing. The pressure to be flawless can paralyze us, preventing us from taking risks and speaking up.

5. **Past traumas or negative experiences:** Previous experiences of discrimination, rejection, or silencing can create internal barriers. We may fear reliving those experiences or worry about opening ourselves up to further harm.

6. **Lack of confidence**: A lack of confidence in our abilities, worth, or the value of our perspectives can hold us back from speaking up. We may question whether we have the right to voice our opinions, leading to silence and inaction.

7. **Fear of confrontation**: Some individuals may avoid speaking up due to a fear of conflict or confrontation. The discomfort of challenging others' viewpoints or engaging in difficult conversations can be an internal barrier that prevents us from taking action.

Acknowledging and addressing our internal obstacles, we tap into our true potential and create a ripple effect of courage and change. These internal obstacles can vary in intensity and may affect individuals differently. Overcoming them requires self-reflection, self-compassion, and a willingness to confront our fears. By addressing these obstacles, we can empower ourselves to speak up, challenge discrimination, and make a difference.

Each of these elements - embracing vulnerability, breaking the silence, and overcoming fear and self-doubt - plays a significant role in our journey toward creating inclusive environments. We become agents of change by sharing our stories, challenging biases, and speaking up against discrimination. We can foster understanding, empower others to share their experiences and build a society that values diversity, inclusivity, and equality.

Practical Actions
1. Reflect on your own experiences and vulnerabilities. Consider how embracing vulnerability can deepen connections and foster understanding.
2. Practice speaking up in situations where you witness injustice or biases. In the succeeding chapters, you will learn some strategies/ tools that will help you be more confident addressing these situations. Develop assertiveness skills and find your voice to advocate for change.

3. Seek support from allies and mentors who can provide guidance and encouragement on your journey to overcoming fear and self-doubt.
4. Foster a growth mindset and embrace the learning process. Recognize that mistakes and failures are opportunities for growth and improvement.
5. Engage in courageous conversations and actively listen to the stories of others. By creating a safe space for vulnerability, we foster empathy and understanding.

Chapter 4
Cultivating Self-Confidence

"Confidence is not 'they will like me.'
Confidence is 'I'll be fine if they don't.'" –
Unknown

When it comes to overcoming discrimination and achieving success, cultivating self-confidence and resilience becomes essential. In this chapter, I want to share with you the power of embracing your identity, nurturing self-worth and belief, turning challenges into opportunities, building your confidence, self-awareness, and personal empowerment, and harnessing your unique strengths. These are the key ingredients that will help you navigate the complexities of the workplace and thrive despite the obstacles you may face.

Embracing Our Identities

Reflecting on my journey, I realize that embracing my identity has been instrumental in building my self-confidence and resilience. Embracing our identities is not about conforming to societal expectations but about celebrating our uniqueness and finding strength in our differences. It is through this celebration that we can tap into a deep sense of authenticity and purpose, leading to personal and professional growth.

According to a study conducted by Rice University, the University of Houston, and George Mason University, "Hiding your true social identity -- race and ethnicity, gender, age, religion, sexual orientation, or a disability -- at work can result in decreased job satisfaction and increased turnover" (Source: Rice University, University of Houston, & George Mason University Study).

Navigating cultural identity in the workplace can be challenging, but it presents an opportunity for growth and understanding. Roberson and Kulik (2007) highlight the importance of acknowledging and respecting cultural differences, as it leads to enhanced creativity, better decision-making, and improved team dynamics.

My career in HR started with an HR assistant role. After a year, I got promoted to an HR consultant role. I was fortunate to join a team that embodied inclusivity and celebrated diverse perspectives. Under the leadership of a manager who encouraged curiosity and understanding of other cultures, our team flourished in an environment that fostered learning, embraced the richness of our individual identities, and fostered genuine connections through shared conversations and understanding.

One of the standout moments occurred during our lunch breaks when our manager would join us, initiating conversations about our backgrounds and experiences. This inclusive lunchtime ritual contrasted my previous workplace, where managers rarely engaged with their teams during breaks. However, in this team, our manager recognized the value of creating an environment where everyone felt seen, heard, and valued. As we gathered around the lunch table, our manager usually kickstarted discussions by asking about our cultural backgrounds and traditions. It was an invitation for each team member to share their unique stories and perspectives. The conversations flowed effortlessly, with genuine curiosity and respect for one another's experiences.

I remember one lunchtime conversation when a colleague shared her immigration journey, opening up about the challenges and triumphs they had encountered. Their vulnerability and willingness to share their personal story created an atmosphere of trust and authenticity.

This open dialogue about our backgrounds allowed us to forge deeper connections and broadened our understanding of one another. We learned about different customs, traditions, and languages, breaking down barriers and fostering a sense of unity within our team.

Through these lunchtime conversations, I discovered the power of genuine engagement and curiosity in fostering inclusivity. Our manager's presence and active participation created a safe space where we could freely express our identities and celebrate our unique backgrounds.

As a result, our team dynamics flourished. We became more than just colleagues; we formed a tight-knit community that supported and uplifted one another. This sense of belonging and acceptance transcended the lunch table and permeated every aspect of our work.

Acts of inclusion are not always about grand gestures or elaborate policies; sometimes, the most transformative moments stem from simple acts of curiosity, authenticity, and genuine human connection.

Leaders who initiate conversations, express genuine curiosity, and actively seek to understand their team members' diverse backgrounds and experiences. Create an environment where everyone feels seen, heard, and valued and where each person's unique contributions are celebrated.

I'm continuously inspired by leaders who have walked the path of authenticity and curiosity, setting an example for others. Their actions remind us that inclusivity starts with each of us as we strive to cultivate empathy, understanding, and a deep appreciation for the rich tapestry of human experiences.

Nurturing Self-Worth and Belief in Your Abilities

One of the internal obstacles we often face is a lack of self-worth and belief in our abilities. I've personally experienced moments of self-doubt and imposter syndrome, where I questioned whether I truly belonged and if I had what it takes to succeed. However, nurturing self-worth and belief is crucial for our growth and empowerment.

Recognizing our inherent worth and valuing our unique contributions can combat imposter syndrome and develop a positive self-image (Bravata et al., 2019).

When I was promoted to a consultant role, I grappled with imposter syndrome in a new role. With new and increased responsibilities came a flood of self-doubt. I constantly questioned myself whether I deserved the promotion and if I could fulfill the expectations placed on me.

During team meetings, I often hesitated to share my ideas, fearing they would be met with skepticism or dismissed as inadequate. I felt everyone else in the room was more knowledgeable and competent than I was. The imposter syndrome had taken hold of my thoughts and eroded my self-worth.

During a mentoring conversation with a senior leader, I realized the impact my self-doubt had on my professional growth. They reminded me of my accomplishments and the skills I had demonstrated throughout my career. They shared their own experiences with imposter syndrome, reassuring me that it was a familiar feeling that many high-achieving individuals face.

With their guidance, I began implementing strategies to nurture my self-worth and belief in my abilities. One key strategy was surrounding myself with a supportive network. I sought peers who believed in me and encouraged my personal and professional development. Their unwavering support served as a reminder that my worth was not determined by the opinions of others but by my own unique strengths and contributions.

Practicing self-compassion also played a significant role in nurturing my self-worth. I learned to acknowledge and accept my limitations and mistakes without harsh self-judgment. Instead of criticizing myself for perceived shortcomings, I approached challenges with kindness and understanding. This shift in perspective allowed me to view setbacks as opportunities for growth and learning rather than validations of my self-doubt.

Another empowering strategy was cultivating empowering self-talk. I consciously replaced negative and self-limiting thoughts with positive affirmations. I reminded myself of past achievements and acknowledged my progress on my journey. Reframing my internal dialogue fostered a more positive self-image and bolstered my belief in my capabilities.

Research supports the transformative impact of nurturing self-worth and belief in our abilities. Bravata et al. (2019) found that developing a positive self-image is essential in combatting imposter syndrome and embracing our authentic selves. It allows us to recognize our inherent worth and value, paving the way for increased confidence and success.

Practical Actions
Techniques to Nurture your Self-worth and Belief in your Abilities:

1. *Supportive Network Assessment:* Evaluate your current network and identify individuals who genuinely support and uplift you. Surround yourself with people who believe in your abilities and inspire you to grow. Identify mentors, friends, or colleagues who can provide guidance, encouragement, and constructive feedback.

2. *Self-Compassion Practice:* Cultivate self-compassion by treating yourself with kindness and understanding. When faced with setbacks or challenges, remember that mistakes are growth opportunities. Practice self-forgiveness and replace self-criticism with self-encouragement. Engage in self-care activities that promote your well-being and nurture a positive self-image.

3. *Empowering Affirmations:* Develop a list of positive affirmations tailored to boost your self-worth and belief. Write down affirmations that resonate with you and reflect your strengths and potential. Repeat them daily, silently or aloud, to reinforce positive self-talk and reshape your internal dialogue.

4. *Visualization Exercises:* Utilize visualization techniques to envision yourself successfully overcoming challenges and achieving your goals. Create mental images of yourself confidently navigating situations that previously

caused self-doubt. Engage all your senses to make the visualization experience more vivid and impactful.

5. ***Celebrating Achievements:*** Take time to celebrate and acknowledge your accomplishments, no matter how small they may seem. Maintain a journal or gratitude list to record your achievements, progress, and moments of personal growth. Reflecting on your successes can boost your self-worth and remind you of your capabilities.

6. ***Personal Growth Plan:*** Create a personal growth and development plan, focusing on areas where you want to build confidence and belief in your abilities. Set specific goals and identify actionable steps to achieve them. Regularly review and adjust your plan as you progress on your journey.

7. ***Mindful Self-Reflection:*** Engage in regular moments of self-reflection to gain insights into your thoughts, emotions, and beliefs. Practice mindfulness techniques such as meditation or journaling to cultivate self-awareness and gain a deeper understanding of your values, strengths, and areas for growth.

Choose the strategies that resonate with you and integrate them into your daily life. Embrace the process of self-discovery and growth and watch as your self-confidence and belief in yourself soar.

Building Your Confidence, Self-Awareness, and Personal Empowerment

Confidence, self-awareness, and personal empowerment are fundamental pillars for navigating the workplace with resilience. They contribute to our ability to overcome challenges, seize opportunities, and thrive in our professional journeys. Research conducted by Judge and Hurst (2007) supports the notion that confidence and self-awareness are closely linked to career success. Individuals with high self-confidence and self-awareness are more likely to take on challenging tasks, seek feedback, and proactively manage their professional development.

Growing up, I was surrounded by criticism and constant comparisons to other family members. I was constantly trying to measure up to their achievements and meet the expectations set by others. This environment fostered my competitive nature, and I became determined to prove myself.

At first, my determination stemmed from a desire to gain validation and approval from others. I would finally earn their praise and recognition if I could outshine my relatives and accomplish extraordinary feats. I poured my energy into achieving success in academics, extracurricular activities, and any endeavor that would prove my worth.

However, as I journeyed through life and gained more experiences, I had a realization that transformed my perspective. I began to understand that my self-worth should not be tied to the opinions or expectations of others. I realized that my true validation and fulfillment should come from within.

This profound shift in mindset liberated me from the shackles of external validation. I no longer felt the need to constantly prove myself to others. Instead, I focused on setting goals, embracing my unique strengths, and charting a path that resonated with my authentic self.

With this newfound clarity, my determination took on a different meaning. It became a driving force to dream big and pursue my passions without being burdened by the need for external validation. I shifted my focus from comparing myself to others to embracing my journey and celebrating my achievements.

This change in perspective allowed me to tap into my true potential and brought a sense of fulfillment and joy to my endeavors. I became more focused, resilient, and determined to achieve my goals for the sheer joy of personal growth and self-fulfillment.

I realized that success is not defined by comparisons or external validation but by fulfilling our dreams and aspirations. By embracing this mindset, I liberated myself from the constraints of others' expectations. I allowed myself to pursue what indeed mattered to me.

This journey taught me the power of self-determination and the importance of focusing on my own path. It was a transformative experience that taught me to trust my abilities, embrace challenges as opportunities for growth, and prioritize my fulfillment and happiness.

Now, I approach every endeavor with a deep sense of determination, not to prove myself to anyone else but to prove to myself that I am capable of achieving greatness. I am driven by my dreams, aspirations, and the knowledge that I can create the life I desire.

Practical Actions
Techniques To Build Confidence, Self-Awareness, and Personal Empowerment
1. ***Embrace Self-Reflection***: Dedicate regular time for self-reflection to gain a deeper understanding of your strengths, areas for improvement, and aspirations. Journaling,

mindfulness practices, and seeking feedback can enhance self-awareness and contribute to personal growth.

2. **Take Calculated Risks:** Stepping out of your comfort zone and taking calculated risks is crucial for personal growth and building confidence. Embrace new challenges, seek opportunities to stretch your capabilities, and learn from successes and failures.

3. **Set Boundaries:** Establish clear boundaries to protect your time, energy, and well-being. Clearly communicate your needs and limitations to colleagues, supervisors, and stakeholders. Prioritize self-care and maintain a healthy work-life balance.

4. **Seek Support and Mentorship:** Surround yourself with a supportive network of colleagues, mentors, and peers who can provide guidance, encouragement, and constructive feedback. Engage in mentorship programs and professional communities to foster personal and professional growth.

5. **Develop Resilient Habits:** Cultivate habits that contribute to your resilience and well-being. Practice self-care, exercise regularly, prioritize sleep, and nurture healthy relationships. Building resilience allows you to bounce back from setbacks and maintain a positive outlook.

By implementing these techniques and embracing the journey of building confidence, self-awareness, and personal empowerment, you can unlock your true potential and navigate the workplace with resilience and purpose. Remember, confidence is not about being free from doubt; it is about acknowledging your abilities, embracing growth, and empowering yourself to take ownership of your professional journey.

Harnessing Your Unique Strengths

Our unique strengths, talents, and skills contribute to our success. Embracing our individual strengths empowers us and enhances the overall success of the team and organization (Avery et al., 2007). Identifying the unique strengths of individuals in a team celebrates the power of diversity and inclusion in the workplace.

A friend and former colleague, a team lead in a pharmaceutical company, was entrusted with planning a high-profile event for their top prescribers. They embarked on this challenging project with a team of six talented individuals, aiming to create a memorable and impactful experience for their esteemed guests.

However, as they delved into the planning process, they encountered various obstacles that tested their skills and teamwork. Tight deadlines, limited resources, and the pressure to deliver a flawless event created a sense of urgency and heightened expectations.

One particular hurdle was coordinating the top prescribers' diverse needs and preferences. Each had unique requirements and expectations, ranging from specific dietary restrictions to preferred presentation formats. They had to meticulously address each request while ensuring a cohesive and engaging event program.

Navigating this complexity required effective communication, adaptability, and keen attention to detail. As the team lead, she facilitated open discussions and encouraged collaboration, valuing the input and expertise of each team member. By leveraging their collective strengths, they were able to develop innovative solutions and overcome challenges with resilience.

Additionally, her role involved fostering solid relationships with key stakeholders, including venue managers, suppliers, and speakers. Building rapport and effectively managing these partnerships was essential in securing the necessary resources and ensuring the event's success.

She witnessed her team members' tremendous growth and development throughout the planning process. Each individual embraced their unique strengths and responsibilities, collaborating seamlessly to bring their shared vision to life. They celebrated their achievements, learned from setbacks, and constantly adapted their plans to create an exceptional event that exceeded expectations.

On the day of the event, as she stood before the room filled with top prescribers, she felt a deep sense of pride and fulfillment. Their collective efforts culminated in a successful event that showcased their company's dedication to excellence and fostered meaningful connections among the attendees.

This experience as a team lead in planning the event for top prescribers taught her the importance of effective leadership, collaboration, and resourcefulness. It reinforced the value of embracing challenges as opportunities for growth and innovation. By harnessing her team's collective strengths, they created a remarkable event that left a lasting impression on the prescribers and strengthened their company's position as a trusted pharmaceutical organization.

In my workshops, I use the **Strengths Identification and Harnessing Worksheet** to assist participants in identifying and harnessing their unique strengths.

This tool guides them through a series of prompts and questions to help them gain clarity on their strengths, reflect on their application, and strategize how to effectively leverage them in their personal and professional lives. Figure 2 will give you a snapshot of the questions in the worksheet.

You can download a copy of the complete worksheet including a guide on how to use them from our website: https://www.theinclusionjourney.com/UnHideYourself

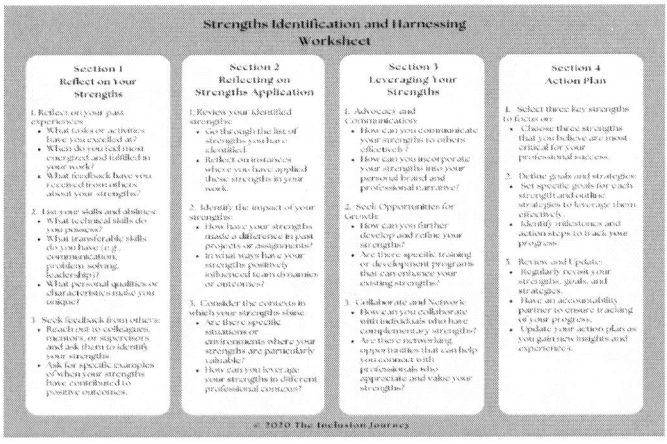

Figure 2: **Strengths Identification and Harnessing Worksheet**

The worksheet is a tool to guide your self-reflection and assist you in harnessing your unique strengths. Use it as a framework to explore and capitalize on your strengths, ultimately empowering you to achieve greater success and fulfillment in your professional life.

Chapter 5
UnHide Yourself Blueprint™

*"Breaking the invisible chain of inequity: bias, stigma, and stereotypes,
we unhide ourselves from society's constraints, stepping into the power of authenticity and empowerment."*
- *Maria N. Drueco*

What if there was a blueprint that could empower you, your team, and your organization to break free from the constraints of bias, stigma, and stereotypes? A blueprint that transforms individuals, fosters inclusive cultures and drives positive change.

As a passionate advocate for diversity, equity, and inclusion, I have always been driven to create positive change in the world. However, it was a personal experience that ignited my desire to create the **UnHide Yourself Blueprint™** and offer it to my clients.

Throughout my various workplace experiences, stereotypes, stigma, biases, microaggressions, discrimination, and racism persist. These issues remain alarmingly prevalent, serving as an important reminder that this is the reality in the daily lives of the people who belong to the marginalized group. It was disheartening to witness talented individuals from this group being silenced and constrained by the systems meant to support them. I saw the immense potential left untapped, and it became clear that something needed to change.

Motivated by a deep sense of purpose, I embarked on a journey of self-reflection and growth. To deepen my knowledge and understanding, I actively pursued opportunities to enhance my awareness. I immersed myself in research, delved into relevant courses, sought expert guidance, and engaged in meaningful conversations with individuals who had experienced similar challenges. Through this continuous process of learning and self-reflection, I realized that creating lasting change required a holistic approach beyond surface-level initiatives.

Driven by the desire to empower others and equipped with valuable knowledge and tools, I meticulously crafted the **UnHide Yourself Blueprint™**.

Just as architects and engineers rely on a blueprint to provide strategic direction for a successful transformation of a building or project, the **UnHide Yourself Blueprint™** serves as a comprehensive and structured guide to facilitate your personal and professional growth. Like a carefully crafted architectural plan, this strategic framework is designed to lead you through a transformative journey, empowering you to break free from the constraints of bias, stigma, and stereotypes.

The 9 steps under each phase are well-defined, empowering individuals and organizations to actively dismantle biases, challenge stereotypes, and foster inclusive environments. It is a roadmap that guides individuals and organizations through a empowering journey of self-discovery, growth, and action, enabling them to create positive change and cultivate inclusive cultures.

I have witnessed firsthand the powerful impact of the **UnHide Yourself Blueprint™** on my clients. From corporate leaders to entrepreneurs, individuals have embraced their unique identities, unlocked their full potential, and created positive change within their organizations and communities. The Blueprint has become a catalyst for empowerment, enabling individuals to challenge discrimination, cultivate inclusive cultures, and build thriving workplaces.

UnHide Yourself™ Blueprint

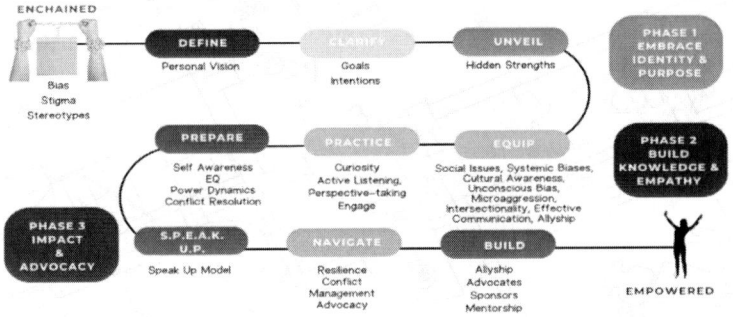

© 2020 The Inclusion Journey

Figure 3: **UnHide Yourself™ Blueprint**

The UnHide Yourself Blueprint™

Step into the **UnHide Yourself Blueprint™**, a comprehensive framework designed to guide individuals, teams, and organizations on a transformative journey towards empowerment, inclusion, and authentic self-expression. This blueprint is designed to liberate you from the constraints of discrimination, bias stigma and stereotypes, empowering you to embrace your authentic self and fearlessly confront the barriers that hinder your growth.

Why would I want to use the UnHide Yourself™ Blueprint?

I get this question from individuals and leaders alike.

The answer is simple.

This blueprint is a powerful catalyst for personal growth, team cohesion, and organizational success. It enables you to unlock your unique strengths, enhance collaboration, and harness the power of diversity. By embracing the **UnHide Yourself Blueprint™,** you can create a workplace where everyone can thrive, contribute their best, and feel valued and respected.

Let me explain further the impact on 4 levels: individual, leadership, team and organization.

Individual Level Impact

For individuals who feel enchained with the weight of biases, limitations, and societal expectations, by following the **UnHide Yourself Blueprint™,** you will gain the tools, mindset, and strategies to challenge discrimination, navigate difficult conversations, and cultivate an inclusive environment where everyone's voices are heard and valued.

This Blueprint is not just about theoretical knowledge; it is a practical roadmap with a holistic approach that empowers you to take meaningful action and drive sustainable change. It provides guidance on embracing your identity, building self-confidence, and developing resilience to overcome obstacles. It equips you with the skills to engage in open and empathetic communication, effectively challenge biases, and foster a culture of inclusion and belonging.

Leadership Level Impact
Leaders who are tired of being enchained by ineffective Diversity, Equity, and Inclusion (DEI) strategies and yearn for a more comprehensive approach that aligns with their vision of a genuinely inclusive workplace can find solace in the **UnHide Yourself Blueprint™**. This transformative roadmap offers a fresh perspective and practical tools to break free from the limitations of traditional DEI approaches and create an environment where all employees can thrive. By embracing the **UnHide Yourself Blueprint™** holistic framework, leaders can pave the way for lasting change, fostering a diversity, equity, and inclusion culture that reflects their vision and empowers their workforce.

You emerge as a visionary leader who breaks free from the constraints of ineffective DEI strategies. You gain the knowledge and tools to revolutionize the organization's approach to diversity, equity, and inclusion. You become empowered to challenge the status quo, leveraging your influence to implement transformative DEI initiatives that drive meaningful change and foster a culture of inclusivity and belonging. As a visionary leader, you set a new standard for DEI in the business world, inspiring others to follow suit and creating a lasting impact in your industry.

Team Level Impact

For fragmented, fragile teams that struggle to meet their objectives, **the UnHide Yourself Blueprint™** helps foster a culture of inclusivity, collaboration, and innovation. Team members become equipped with the knowledge and skills to challenge biases, embrace diversity, and engage in open and respectful communication. This shift in mindset and behavior creates an environment where everyone's perspectives are valued and heard.

Organizational Level Impact

For organizations that have initiated diversity, equity, and inclusion efforts and made some progress but struggle with implementation, employee engagement, and sustaining long-term impact or those who seek to innovate further, drive systemic change, and make a broader impact beyond their walls, the **UnHide Yourself Blueprint™,** will help undergo a profound transformation to achieve a culture of empowerment and inclusion. They become a role model in the industry and positively impact society.

The **UnHide Yourself Blueprint™** empowers you and your team to create positive change from within. It enables you to build an environment where individuals can thrive, contribute their unique perspectives, and feel a sense of belonging. By embracing this transformative journey, you and your organization become catalysts for broader societal change, breaking down barriers and creating a more equitable and inclusive world.

*Disclaimer: It is important to note that the practical actions for each step of the **UnHide Yourself Blueprint™** mentioned in the following pages of this book are not an exhaustive list but a starting point for immediate action. The **UnHide Yourself Blueprint™** is a proprietary methodology I use with clients that offers a comprehensive approach beyond these initial steps, providing a framework for deeper exploration and implementation. While you can begin incorporating these steps into your life* *and work right away, the blueprint, when delivered as a methodology, offers a broader range of strategies, exercises, and resources to support your personal growth and transformation. It encourages ongoing learning, reflection, and adaptation to meet the unique needs of individuals and organizations.*

3 Phases to UnHide Yourself (The UnHide™ Yourself Blueprint)

The **UnHide Yourself Blueprint™** is a well-structured framework that guides individuals and organizations through a transformative journey toward empowerment and positive change. It consists of three distinct phases, each designed to facilitate a specific transformational outcome. Within each phase, three essential steps act as building blocks for progress and growth.

Phase 1: Embracing Identity and Purpose

This initial phase focuses on self-discovery and clarifying personal vision. Through three essential steps:

1. *Define Personal Vision*
2. *Clarify Your Goals and Intentions*
3. *Unveiling Your Hidden Strengths*

During this phase, individuals embark on a journey of uncovering their authentic identity, setting meaningful goals, and recognizing their unique abilities.

Transformation: From Uncertain to Focused

Phase 2: Building Knowledge and Empathy
The second phase of the blueprint centers around developing a deeper understanding of biases and systemic issues and fostering empathy. It comprises three pivotal steps:

4. *Equipping Yourself with Knowledge*
5. *Practicing Active Listening and Empathy*
6. *Preparing for Courageous Conversations*

These steps empower individuals to expand their knowledge, enhance communication skills, and engage in meaningful conversations that challenge biases and promote understanding.

Transformation: From Developing Awareness to Empathetic Courage

Phase 3: Impact and Advocacy
The final phase focuses on empowering individuals to become advocates for change and create a lasting impact. It consists of three critical steps:

7. *Speaking Up with Confidence and Impact*
8. *Navigating Resistance and Repercussions*
9. *Building Supportive Alliances*

These steps enable individuals to express themselves confidently, navigate challenges and setbacks, and foster collaborative relationships that drive positive change.

Transformation: From Self-Doubt to Empowered Advocacy

Let's dive deeper into each of the steps:

Phase 1

Step 1: Define Your Vision
Transformation: From feeling uncertain about your direction to having a clear sense of purpose and direction in your personal and professional life.
In the cluttered and fast-paced world, we live in, it's easy to lose sight of our true desires and aspirations. Step 1 of the **UnHide Yourself Blueprint™** is designed to help you declutter your mind and define your vision. This crucial

first step sets the foundation for your transformative journey toward empowerment and positive change.

This step is about clarifying your vision, which involves reflecting on your values, passions, and aspirations. It's about understanding what you want to achieve and who you want to become. By defining your vision, you create a guiding light that directs your actions and decisions. It gives you a sense of purpose and clarity, helping you stay focused on what truly matters to you.

Without a clear vision, you may feel lost, uncertain, and lacking direction in your personal and professional life. You may find it challenging to make decisions or take actions that align with your authentic self.

People often neglect this step or settle for vague, generic visions lacking specificity and meaning. They may also struggle to articulate their vision due to self-doubt or fear of failure.

During Step 1, you'll embark on a reflective process that invites you to dive deep into your values, passions, and aspirations. Through introspection and self-discovery exercises, you'll peel away the layers of external influences and societal expectations to uncover your authentic desires.

By dedicating time and attention to defining your vision, you gain clarity about what truly matters to you. You'll identify what you want to achieve and who you aspire to become. This process creates a guiding light that illuminates your path, guiding your actions and decisions with purpose and intention. You'll gain valuable insights into your true desires, dreams, and goals. You'll explore your values and passions, allowing them to inform and shape your vision. You'll uncover your unique aspirations set a clear and compelling direction for your life.

Defining your vision is not a one-time event but an ongoing process of self-discovery and refinement. The **UnHide Yourself Blueprint™** provides the tools and exercises to continually revisit and refine your vision as you grow and evolve.

Completing Step 1 and defining your personal vision lays a solid foundation for your transformative journey. You'll experience a sense of clarity and purpose that will guide you through the remaining steps of the blueprint. With a defined personal vision, you gain the confidence and motivation to take meaningful action toward your desired life.

Remember, Step 1 is just the beginning. It sets the stage for your personal growth and empowerment, paving the way for the transformative journey ahead.

Practical Actions:

- Set aside dedicated time for self-reflection and introspection.
- Write down your values, passions, and aspirations.
- Create a vision statement that encapsulates your desired future.
- Break down your vision into smaller, actionable goals.

Step 2: Clarify Your Goals and Intentions

Transformation: From being overwhelmed or directionless to having a focused roadmap for achieving your vision.

Having a vision without concrete goals is like having a destination without a roadmap. In Step 2 of **the UnHide Yourself Blueprint™,** we dive deeper into clarifying your goals and intentions. This step transforms your overarching vision into actionable steps that propel you forward on your transformative journey.

Goals are the building blocks of your vision, providing a clear direction and purpose. By breaking down your vision into specific, measurable, achievable, relevant, and time-bound (SMART) goals, you create a roadmap that guides your actions and keeps you focused on what truly matters to you.

Without clear goals, you may feel aimless and struggle to make meaningful progress. You might find it challenging to stay focused and easily get distracted by other priorities or lose motivation.

People often set vague or unrealistic goals, making measuring progress or maintaining motivation difficult. They may also fail to align their goals with their values and vision, leading to a lack of fulfillment or satisfaction.

During this phase, we explore effective strategies for goal setting and provide you with practical tools to help you define meaningful objectives. You create a sense of purpose and direction in your life by aligning your goals with your values and vision. Each goal becomes a stepping stone that brings you closer to realizing your vision.

Clarifying your goals and intentions empowers you to:

- **Create focus:** By clearly defining your goals, you gain clarity on your goals and the steps required to get there. This focus helps you make decisions and prioritize your actions, ensuring you stay on track toward your vision.

- **Establish accountability**: Setting specific and measurable goals provides a benchmark for tracking progress. It holds you accountable and motivates you to take consistent action toward achieving your aspirations.
- **Maintain motivation:** Goals serve as a source of motivation and inspiration. When you have clear intentions, you have a compelling reason to persevere, even when faced with challenges or setbacks.

By engaging in Step 2 of the **UnHide Yourself Blueprint™,** you unlock the power of clarifying your goals and intentions. This process propels you forward, transforming your vision into a practical and achievable plan. In Chapter 8, I share the S.U.C.C.E.S.S. framework, a powerful tool to set goals and commit to it is. You can refer to this as you set SMART goals that align with your values and vision, you gain the focus, accountability, and motivation necessary to realize your true potential.

Practical Actions:
- Review and refine your vision statement.
- Set specific, measurable, achievable, relevant, and time-bound (SMART) goals.

- Prioritize your goals and identify key milestones.
- Develop an action plan with clear steps to achieve your goals.

Step 3: Unveiling Your Hidden Strengths

Transformation: From underestimating your abilities to recognizing and leveraging your unique strengths.

Within each of us lies a treasure trove of untapped potential and hidden strengths. In Step 3 of the **UnHide Yourself Blueprint™,** we embark on a transformative journey of self-discovery, uncovering the unique talents, skills, and abilities that have remained concealed or underappreciated. This step is about shedding light on the qualities that make you exceptional and recognizing their value to your personal and professional life.

Unveiling your hidden strengths allows you to unleash your full potential and maximize your impact. It helps you build on your natural talents and abilities, leading to greater self-belief and success in achieving your goals.

You must uncover your hidden strengths to ensure you know valuable assets that could contribute to your personal and professional growth. Otherwise, you may miss opportunities for success and fulfillment.

People often focus more on their weaknesses rather than embracing and leveraging their strengths. They may overlook their unique talents or downplay their accomplishments, leading to a lack of self-confidence and underutilization of their potential.

Unveiling your hidden strengths empowers you in several ways:

- **Boosting self-confidence:** Discovering your strengths provides a powerful confidence boost. As you become aware of your unique talents and abilities, you gain a newfound belief in your capabilities. This self-assurance enables you to take on challenges with conviction and tackle them head-on.
- **Enhancing effectiveness:** By leveraging your strengths, you can maximize your effectiveness in various areas of your life. When you align your tasks and responsibilities with your natural talents, you work in a state of flow, achieving higher levels of productivity and satisfaction.
- **Unlocking success:** Harnessing your strengths unlocks your true potential and sets you on a trajectory toward success. When you leverage your innate abilities, you tap into your authentic self, enabling you to thrive and achieve remarkable outcomes.

This step in the **UnHide Yourself Blueprint™** empowers you to embrace your strengths and leverage them as catalysts for personal and professional success. By unveiling your hidden strengths, you unlock a world of possibilities and embark on a journey of self-realization and fulfillment.

Practical Actions:

- Conduct a self-assessment to identify your strengths. Use the ***Strengths Identification and Harnessing Worksheet Questions*** mentioned in Chapter 4.
- Seek feedback from colleagues, mentors, or trusted individuals.
- Reflect on past accomplishments and identify the skills that contributed to your success.
- Develop a plan to further develop and apply your strengths in your professional life.

Phase 2
Step 4: Equipping Yourself with Knowledge

Transformation: From being unaware of biases and systemic issues to being well-informed and equipped to challenge them.

Knowledge is a crucial driver of personal growth and transformation. In Step 4, we strongly emphasize equipping ourselves with the necessary knowledge and understanding to navigate the complexities of bias, discrimination, and challenging conversations.

To create meaningful change, staying informed about social issues, diversity, equity, and inclusion is essential. Expanding our knowledge deepens our understanding of different perspectives, cultures, and systemic biases. This knowledge empowers us to engage in informed conversations, challenge biases, and advocate for change effectively.

Without knowledge and understanding, you may unintentionally perpetuate biases, contribute to discriminatory practices, or remain unaware of the systemic issues that hinder inclusivity. You may struggle to engage in meaningful conversations or create positive change effectively.

People may rely on limited or outdated information, failing to seek new knowledge and insights continuously. They may also resist confronting uncomfortable truths or be hesitant to question their existing beliefs or assumptions.

When I work with clients, this stage usually involves a deep dive into various topics that expand knowledge and understanding. By exploring these areas, individuals gain valuable insights and perspectives contributing to their personal and professional growth.

Here are some of the topics we delve into during this step:

- **Social Issues and Systemic Biases**: Examine the underlying causes of social issues and delve into the systemic biases perpetuating inequities. By gaining a deeper understanding of these issues, you can identify opportunities for intervention and contribute to creating more inclusive environments.
- **Cultural Awareness and Sensitivity**: Cultural awareness and sensitivity is important in fostering inclusivity. By exploring different cultural norms, practices, and perspectives, you can engage with diverse individuals and communities respectfully and inclusively.
- **Unconscious Bias and Stereotypes**: Learn about and identify ways you can address the impact of unconscious biases and stereotypes on our perceptions and interactions. You can challenge and mitigate their influence by raising awareness of these biases and fostering more inclusive and unbiased environments.
- **Intersectionality**: The concept of intersectionality recognizes the interconnected nature of various social identities and the unique challenges faced by individuals who belong to marginalized groups. Understanding intersectionality helps you navigate the

complexities of identity and fosters greater empathy and inclusivity.

- **Effective Communication and Active Listening**: Learn different strategies promoting inclusivity, such as active listening, open-mindedness, and empathetic communication. These skills will enable you to engage in meaningful and respectful conversations, even in challenging circumstances.
- **Strategies for Allyship and Advocacy:** Allyship and advocacy are essential in creating change. By equipping yourself with strategies to be influential allies, you can support marginalized individuals and amplify their voices, working together to dismantle systemic barriers.

While our workshops and training programs provide a structured learning environment, I still encourage individuals to explore these topics independently. Educating yourself on these subjects can further enhance your understanding and contribute to your growth. There are numerous books, articles, podcasts, and online resources available that can provide valuable insights into these critical areas.

By dedicating time and effort to expand your knowledge, you will be better equipped to navigate the complexities of bias, discrimination, and difficult conversations. It is an ongoing self-education and continuous learning process that will empower you to impact your personal and professional spheres positively.

Practical Actions:
- Stay informed about current social issues, diversity, equity, and inclusion topics.
- Read books, articles, and research papers on relevant subjects.
- Attend workshops, webinars, or conferences on diversity and inclusion.
- Engage in conversations and seek diverse perspectives on social issues.

Step 5: Practicing Active Listening and Empathy

Transformation: From passive listening to active listening and empathetic communication.

At the heart of effective communication lies the ability to truly listen and empathize with others. In this transformative step, we delve into the art of active listening and empathy, honing our skills to foster understanding and build stronger connections. By practicing active listening, we open ourselves to genuinely hearing and comprehending what others are saying, creating a safe space for open dialogue and mutual respect.

Without active listening and empathy, communication may be shallow, misunderstandings may arise, and relationships may suffer. A lack of empathy can lead to disconnection, conflict, and understanding between individuals or groups.

People may engage in passive listening, where they hear but don't truly understand or acknowledge others' experiences. They may also struggle to step out of their perspectives or prioritize their viewpoints over those of others.

During this step, there are various techniques and strategies that you can explore to enhance your listening skills and deepen your capacity for empathy.

Here are some key aspects to delve into:

- **Paraphrasing and Summarizing:** Learn the power of paraphrasing and summarizing to ensure accurate understanding. Restating others' ideas in our own words confirms our comprehension and shows our genuine interest in their perspective.
- **Clarifying and Asking Questions:** By seeking clarity, we avoid misunderstandings and allow for a deeper exploration of ideas. Thoughtful questions demonstrate our engagement and encourage others to share more of their thoughts and feelings.

- **Reflecting and Validating Emotions:** When we learn to reflect on the emotions expressed by others, we validate their experiences. Acknowledging their feelings creates a supportive environment where individuals feel heard and understood.
- **Nonverbal Communication:** Nonverbal cues, such as body language, facial expressions, and tone of voice, if not done properly can create a negative impact. Understanding how to interpret and respond to these signals helps us attune to others' emotions and intentions.

To deepen our empathy, we engage in various exercises and activities that foster a genuine understanding of others' experiences and perspectives. These may include storytelling, role-playing, or guided discussions that allow us to step into others' shoes and see the world from their point of view.

By cultivating active listening and empathy, we unlock the power to forge meaningful connections and build bridges of understanding. We create a space where diverse voices are valued, fostering an inclusive environment where everyone feels seen, heard, and respected. Through this practice, we can bridge divides, resolve conflicts, and nurture deeper connections within our personal and professional relationships.

Dedicating time and effort to practicing active listening and empathy will enhance your communication abilities, nurture empathy, and foster a more inclusive and connected world.

Practical Actions:
- Practice active listening techniques, such as paraphrasing and reflecting.
- Develop empathy through perspective-taking exercises.
- Engage in deep conversations with colleagues or friends to understand their experiences and perspectives.
- Show genuine interest and curiosity when engaging with others.

Step 6: Preparing for Courageous Conversations
Transformation: From avoiding difficult conversations to feeling prepared and confident in addressing sensitive topics.

Courageous conversations are pivotal moments that allow us to address sensitive and challenging topics head-on. While these conversations may feel daunting, we can navigate them effectively and create positive change with proper preparation and continuous learning.

Preparing for courageous conversations allows you to advocate for yourself and others, challenge the status quo, and drive positive change. It helps you navigate difficult discussions with confidence, empathy, and a focus on finding common ground.

Difficult conversations may become unproductive, confrontational, or even damaging without preparation. Important issues may remain unaddressed, perpetuating biases and creating an environment that isn't inclusive.

People may avoid difficult conversations altogether due to fear, discomfort, or uncertainty. They may also lack the necessary skills to navigate power dynamics, manage emotions, or approach sensitive topics with sensitivity and respect.

Courageous conversations are necessary when sensitive or challenging topics must be addressed. Here are some examples of situations that may warrant a courageous conversation:

- **Addressing bias and discrimination:** When you witness or experience instances of bias, discrimination, or microaggressions, it's important to have courageous conversations to challenge these behaviors and promote inclusivity.

- **Resolving conflicts:** If there are unresolved conflicts or tensions within a team or between individuals, courageous conversations can help address the issues, explore different perspectives, and work towards finding a resolution.
- **Providing feedback:** Giving honest and constructive feedback, especially when it may be uncomfortable or sensitive, requires courage. Courageous conversations facilitate growth and improvement by addressing areas for development or performance concerns.
- **Advocating for change:** When you recognize systemic issues or areas of improvement within an organization or community, courageous conversations can be a means to advocate for change, share ideas, and promote positive transformation.
- **Discussing challenging or controversial topics:** Engaging in conversations about topics typically considered difficult or controversial, such as politics, social issues, or sensitive matters, can create opportunities for understanding, bridge gaps, and foster meaningful dialogue.
- **Addressing power dynamics:** Courageous conversations can help address power imbalances, whether within a team, an organization, or society. It involves discussing

and challenging the unequal distribution of power and advocating for equity and fairness.

Courageous conversations require sensitivity, respect, active listening, and a willingness to engage in dialogue that may be uncomfortable or challenging. They serve as catalysts for growth, understanding, and positive change.
During this stage, we recognize that courageous conversations require a deliberate and intentional approach. We delve into strategies that enable us to prepare ourselves for engaging in these crucial discussions. By attending training and workshops focused specifically on courageous conversations, we acquire the tools, techniques, and mindset necessary to navigate these interactions with confidence and impact.

In Step 6, the emphasis is on developing the skills necessary to engage in courageous conversations effectively. The skills include:

- **Self-Awareness:** Understanding our own beliefs, biases, and triggers is crucial before engaging in courageous conversations. We explore self-reflection exercises and engage in activities that help us develop a deeper understanding of ourselves and how our perspectives may influence the conversation.
- **Emotional Intelligence:** Developing emotional intelligence is essential for managing our own emotions and understanding the emotions of

others during courageous conversations. We learn techniques to regulate our emotions, empathize with others, and cultivate a safe and supportive environment for dialogue.

- **Active Listening and Empathy:** Active listening and empathy play a vital role in courageous conversations. We explore techniques to enhance our listening skills, such as paraphrasing, summarizing, and reflecting back the speaker's message. We also learn to cultivate empathy and deepen our understanding of others' experiences and perspectives.

- **Constructive Communication:** Effective communication is essential for productive and respectful conversations. We delve into assertive communication techniques, learning how to express our thoughts and ideas with clarity, confidence, and impact. We also explore methods for providing constructive feedback and managing conflicts constructively.

- **Navigating Power Dynamics:** Courageous conversations often involve navigating power dynamics, which can impact the flow and outcomes of the conversation. We learn strategies to address power imbalances, ensure equitable participation, and create a safe space where everyone's voice is heard and valued.

- **Conflict Resolution:** Courageous conversations may bring forth disagreements and conflicts. We explore strategies for managing conflicts constructively, seeking common ground, and finding mutually beneficial solutions. By developing conflict resolution skills, we can foster understanding and collaboration even in challenging situations.

Attending training and workshops focused on courageous conversations provides a transformative experience. The setting provides a structured and guided approach to dive deep into the essential skill set of courageous conversation, deepen our knowledge, practice in a safe environment and gain valuable insights from experienced facilitators and peers. By investing in our growth and development in this area, we become more confident and effective in engaging in courageous conversations that challenge bias, discrimination, and injustice.

Courageous conversation is a skill that evolves and strengthens with practice and continuous learning.

I encourage you to seek relevant training and workshops that align with your growth objectives. If you're a leader and looking to have this training be part of your employee or leader's development, feel free to contact me by email: maria@theinclusionjourney.com

Practical Actions:

1. Identify potential challenging conversations: Recognize situations or topics that require addressing sensitive or difficult issues for positive change.

2. Prepare emotionally: Reflect on your emotions and mindset and develop strategies to manage them during challenging conversations. This may involve deep breathing exercises, mindfulness techniques, or self-reflection practices.

3. Clarify intentions: Define the purpose and desired outcome of the conversation. Clarify your goals, whether it's to foster understanding, challenge biases, or seek resolution.

4. Gather information: Conduct research and gather relevant facts and data to support your viewpoints and arguments. This will enhance your credibility and strengthen your position during the conversation.

5. Practice active listening: Cultivate active listening skills by focusing on the speaker, maintaining eye contact, and avoiding interruptions. Show genuine curiosity and seek to understand their perspective without judgment.

6. Develop empathy: Put yourself in the other person's shoes and strive to understand their experiences, emotions, and motivations. Practice empathy to foster connection and create a safe space for dialogue.

7. Use respectful and assertive communication: Express your thoughts, opinions, and concerns assertively and respectfully. Clearly articulate your viewpoints while actively inviting and valuing the perspectives of others. In the next step, I will share the **S.P.E.A.K.U.P. Model**, a framework you can use that'll help you develop confidence speaking up.

8. Manage conflict constructively: Learn conflict resolution strategies to navigate disagreements and challenges. Develop skills in finding common ground, seeking compromise, and maintaining respectful dialogue.

9. Seek support and feedback: Engage with a trusted mentor, coach, or peer who can provide guidance, feedback, and support as you prepare for courageous conversations. They can offer valuable insights and help refine your approach.

Phase 3
Step 7: Speaking Up with Confidence and Impact
Transformation: From staying silent to expressing your thoughts and ideas confidently and positively.

Building upon the foundation laid by the previous steps, Step 7 of the **UnHide Yourself Blueprint™** delves into the essential skill of speaking up with confidence and impact. This step is crucial in empowering individuals to express themselves authentically and effectively communicate their thoughts, ideas, and concerns.

Speaking up with confidence and impact amplifies your voice, enables you to share your perspectives and ideas, and contributes to positive change. It helps you influence others, build credibility, and create meaningful connections.

When you don't speak up, your ideas and contributions may go unheard, hindering personal and professional growth. Lack of confidence or ineffective communication may limit your ability to create the desired impact.

People may struggle with self-doubt, fear of judgment, or difficulty expressing themselves assertively. They may overlook the power of storytelling or fail to engage their audience effectively when communicating their thoughts or ideas.

You may have noticed that both Step 6 and Step 7 involve effective communication.

Step 6 focuses on preparing for and engaging in challenging conversations. In contrast, Step 7 emphasizes the skills needed for self-expression and making a lasting impact through effective communication. It focuses on developing the skills and confidence to express oneself assertively and make a positive impact through effective communication.

In Step 7, we focus on speaking up with confidence and impact, honing the skills needed to address bias and inequity effectively:

- Building self-assurance: Cultivating self-confidence and managing self-doubt.
- Authentic expression: Communicating with authenticity and sincerity.
- Assertive communication: Expressing thoughts, needs, and boundaries clearly and respectfully.
- Impactful messaging: Crafting messages that resonate and evoke the desired response.

These skills empower individuals to share their ideas, opinions, and perspectives confidently, bridging the gaps and dismantling biases. By delivering their messages with clarity, conviction, and influence, they create a lasting positive impact on their audience and contribute to a more inclusive and equitable world.

The S.P.E.A.K.U.P. Model

Amidst the multifaceted dynamics of today's organizations and society, the systems we have in place were not inherently designed to accommodate the diverse experiences of people of color and members of marginalized groups. Historically, these voices have been marginalized and silenced, leading to a lack of representation in decision-making processes and perpetuating systemic biases. As a result, many individuals from these communities find it difficult to speak up and initiate courageous conversations.

As I ventured into the diversity, equity, and inclusion work, I recognized the need for a tool that could empower individuals to have courageous conversations even in challenging and potentially unsafe environments.

Through extensive research, personal experiences, and insights gained from working with diverse clients, I developed and refined a conversation tool to navigate crucial discussions confidently and without blame—the **S.P.EA.K.U.P. Model** (Figure 4).

While there may be other models or frameworks that address similar concepts or goals, the uniqueness of the **S.P.EA.K.U.P. Model** lies in its combination and integration of diverse elements from various fields (intercultural communication, psychology and conflict resolution), tailored explicitly to address bias and inequalities in the workplace and society. While some existing models may primarily focus on communication or conflict resolution only, the **S.P.EA.K.U.P. Model** goes beyond the conventional boundaries. It incorporates elements of self-reflection, empathetic listening, and constructive articulation, creating a well-rounded and holistic approach to navigating courageous conversations and advocating for change.

The **S.P.EA.K.U.P. Model's** adaptability and flexibility allow it to be applied in various settings, from corporate boardrooms to community gatherings, making it an invaluable tool for individuals, leaders, and advocates seeking to create lasting and impactful change.

The S.P.EA.K.U.P. Model:
- Provides a structured and supportive approach for navigating difficult discussions, even in vulnerable or unheard spaces.
- Designed as a beacon of empowerment, it helps individuals overcome the fear of backlash, dismissal, or marginalization.
- The model enables individuals to reclaim their voices and challenge biases confidently.

Ready to amplify your voice and navigate courageous conversations?

Let's uncover the power of the S.P.EA.K.U.P.
Model!

S.P.E.A.K.U.P.

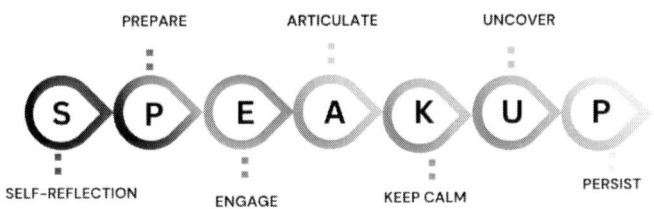

Figure 4: **S.P.E.A.K.U.P. Model**

Let's look at the elements of the **S.P.E.A.K.U.P.
Model:**

S.P.E.A.K. U.P.
1.   **S - Start with Self-reflection**: Before
speaking up, take time to reflect on your own
thoughts, emotions, and intentions. Understand
your motivations for speaking up and ensure
that your message is coming from a place of
authenticity and fairness.
2.   **P - Prepare and Plan:** Plan your
conversation in advance. Consider the specific
issue you want to address, gather relevant
information, and outline your key talking points.

Anticipate potential responses or objections and prepare counterarguments or supportive evidence.

3. **E - Engage in Empathetic Listening**: When engaging in a courageous conversation, actively listen to the other person's perspective. Show empathy and seek to understand their point of view. This helps foster an open and respectful dialogue, increasing the likelihood of a constructive outcome.

4. **A - Articulate with Clarity:** Clearly articulate your thoughts and concerns using clear and concise language. Use "I" statements to express your personal experiences and feelings, while also focusing on the objective facts and impacts of bias. Be confident and assertive in delivering your message.

5. **K - Keep Calm and Composed:** Maintain composure and emotional control during the conversation. Stay calm, even if faced with resistance or challenges. This helps to keep the discussion focused and productive, increasing the chances of a positive outcome.

6. **U - Uncover Solutions:** Collaborate with the other person to find common ground and explore potential solutions. Work together to identify actionable steps that can address bias and promote fairness in hiring and promotion practices. Encourage open dialogue and mutual understanding.

7. **P - Persist and Follow-up:** Advocate for continued change by following up on the

conversation. Monitor progress, ensure that agreed-upon actions are implemented, and hold individuals accountable. Be persistent in your efforts to create a more inclusive and equitable workplace.

I have integrated the **S.P.EA.K.U.P. Model** into consulting, coaching, training, and workshops. Through the transformative journey of the **S.P.EA.K.U.P. Model**, clients have discovered unwavering confidence that guides them gracefully and assertively through challenging discussions. Embracing their unique perspectives, they now express themselves authentically, fostering deeper connections and cultivating more constructive dialogues with their colleagues.

With a focus on self-reflection, preparation, and empathetic listening, they have transformed their approach to courageous conversations, igniting positive change. Successfully unearthing solutions, they have taken meaningful steps towards a more inclusive and equitable workplace.

With newfound clarity and composure, they navigate complexities with ease, embracing collaborative problem-solving to drive lasting impact and create a harmonious and thriving organizational culture. The **S.P.EA.K.U.P.**

Model has empowered my clients to become catalysts of change as they advocate for fairness and inclusion, leaving an indelible mark on their personal and professional spheres.

I take pride in supporting my clients as they advocate for change and hold themselves and others accountable. Together, we celebrate the progress made and continuously strive for a workplace that values and respects the diverse voices and experiences within it.

How can we start meaningful change and create a more inclusive and equitable world? *With one courageous conversation at a time.*

" With each courageous conversation, we confront inequity and embrace diverse perspectives, creating an environment where everyone's voice is heard and valued. Our collective impact becomes unstoppable as these conversations multiply, shaping a more inclusive and equitable landscape within organizations and society. We amplify voices, challenge norms, and break down barriers, fostering a powerful ripple effect of positive transformation. Together, we forge a path towards a brighter, more inclusive future— one courageous conversation at a time."

Maria Drueco

Practical Action:

- Start using and practicing the **S.P.EA.K.U.P. Model** as a tool for courageous conversation.

Step 8: Navigating Resistance and Repercussions

Transformation: From feeling overwhelmed by resistance and setbacks to effectively managing conflicts and staying resilient.

Speaking up and challenging the status quo often comes with resistance and potential repercussions. This step equips individuals with strategies and skills to effectively navigate these situations.

Navigating resistance and repercussions allows you to overcome obstacles, maintain your focus, and continue advocating for positive change. It helps you address objections, constructively manage conflicts, and confidently navigate challenging situations.

Without the ability to navigate resistance and repercussions, you may face setbacks, lose momentum, or even be deterred from challenging biases and pursuing positive change. Essential issues may remain unaddressed, and progress may stagnate.

People may avoid or mishandle resistance, leading to increased conflict, strained relationships, or retreating from their goals. They may struggle to effectively manage objections, address pushback, or assert their viewpoints in challenging situations.

The key elements involved in Step 8 include:

- **Understanding Resistance and Conflict:**
  - Explore the different forms of resistance and conflict that may arise when challenging the status quo.
  - Gain insights into the underlying causes of resistance and how to address them constructively.
- **Developing Resilience:**
  - Learn techniques to build personal resilience, allowing you to navigate setbacks and focus on your goals.
  - Cultivate a growth mindset that sees challenges as opportunities for learning and growth.
- **Strategic Approaches to Conflict Management:**
  - Acquire strategies to manage conflicts and handle objections effectively.
  - Learn how to address pushback and counterarguments constructively and assertively.
- **Advocating for Yourself and Others:**
  - Develop the skills to advocate for yourself and others in challenging situations.
  - Discover effective ways to communicate your viewpoints, demonstrate the value of your ideas, and advocate for positive change.

By engaging with these strategies and developing resilience and a strategic mindset, you can effectively navigate resistance, manage conflicts, and cope with potential negative outcomes. This step empowers you to focus on your goals, push for positive change, and continue advocating for inclusivity and equity in your personal and professional lives.

Practical Actions:

- Enhance your communication skills by practicing active listening, empathy, and non-violent communication techniques.
- Learn to express your thoughts and ideas clearly, assertively, and respectfully, even in challenging situations.
- Develop advocacy skills to effectively communicate your viewpoints, stand up for yourself and others, and promote positive change.
- Learn negotiation techniques to find common ground, build consensus, and address concerns constructively and collaboratively.
- Cultivate emotional intelligence by increasing your self-awareness, managing your emotions, and understanding the emotions of others.
- Learn techniques to regulate emotions, stay calm under pressure, and respond thoughtfully in challenging situations.

- Explore conflict transformation approaches beyond traditional win-lose scenarios and seek mutually beneficial outcomes.
- Learn about restorative justice, mediation, and reconciliation practices to transform conflicts into opportunities for growth and understanding.
- Strengthen your resilience by adopting a growth mindset, embracing challenges as learning opportunities, and bouncing back from setbacks.
- Cultivate a positive mindset by focusing on gratitude, practicing affirmations, and visualizing successful outcomes.

Step 9: Building Supportive Alliances

Transformation: From feeling isolated to creating a network of supportive individuals who share your commitment to diversity and inclusion.

In the final step, we emphasize the importance of building supportive alliances. Surrounding ourselves with like-minded individuals who share our commitment to diversity, equity, and inclusion is crucial for ongoing support and encouragement. It involves creating connections, fostering collaborations, and cultivating a community of like-minded individuals committed to positive change.

Building supportive alliances provides a network of support, inspiration, and shared resources. It enhances your ability to create collective impact, sustain motivation, and navigate challenges with the backing of a supportive ecosystem.

Without supportive alliances, you may feel isolated, unsupported, or overwhelmed in pursuing positive change. Building a community can foster resilience, provide diverse perspectives, and offer opportunities for collaboration and learning.

People may underestimate the power of building relationships and connections, limiting their potential impact. They may fail to seek support or engage in collaborative efforts, hindering their ability to create lasting change and expand their reach.

Practical Actions:

- Attend networking events or join professional groups focused on diversity and inclusion.
- Seek out mentorship opportunities with individuals who align with your values and goals.
- Explore collaborative projects with like-minded individuals and organizations.
- Actively engage in allyship by supporting and advocating for others.

- Look for ways to seek mentorship from experienced professionals who can guide and support you, as well as the benefits of offering mentorship to others, fostering a sense of reciprocity and growth within your network.

The UnHide Yourself Blueprint™ paves the way for an extraordinary transformation from feeling enchained to becoming empowered. This comprehensive framework guides you through a journey of self-discovery, growth, and action, unlocking your true potential and empowering you to challenge biases, cultivate inclusivity, and create positive change.

Throughout this transformative journey, you will redefine your vision, clarify your goals, unveil your hidden strengths, equip yourself with knowledge, practice active listening and empathy, prepare for courageous conversations, speak up with confidence and impact, navigate resistance and repercussions, and build supportive alliances. Each step is a crucial building block that propels you closer to your ultimate transformation – *a transformation that liberates you from the chains of self-doubt, societal barriers, and limited beliefs.*

As you embrace the **UnHide Yourself Blueprint™,** you will witness a profound shift within yourself, your team, your organization, and the world around you. You will emerge confident and courageous, fearlessly challenging the status quo and advocating for a more inclusive and equitable society. Your team will become a cohesive and empowered force, driving innovation, collaboration, and success. Your organization will thrive as it embraces diversity, fosters inclusivity, and reaps the benefits of a truly empowered workforce.

So, I encourage you to embark on this transformative journey, where you break free from the chains that bind you and rise as an empowered changemaker. Unleash your true potential, create a ripple of positive change, and contribute to a world where everyone is valued, heard, and respected.

> **The power to transform yourself and the world lies within you. Embrace it, embrace your journey, and unlock your boundless potential.**
>
> Maria Drueco

Chapter 6: Applying Courageous Conversations

"Advocating for systemic change requires the courage to challenge existing structures and policies. Through courageous conversations, we can shed light on systemic injustices and work towards creating a more just and inclusive society."
- *Maria N. Drueco*

In today's diverse and complex workplaces, courageous conversations are crucial for fostering inclusion, dismantling biases, and creating a more equitable environment.

In this chapter, we dive into the practical application of courageous conversations across various workplace scenarios. Our exploration includes:

- Addressing bias in hiring and promotion processes.
- Responding to microaggressions and stereotypes.
- Navigating discrimination from superiors.
- Advocating for systemic change.

Courageous conversations are not limited to individuals who directly experience bias or discrimination. They are equally essential for leaders and allies who want to actively contribute to creating a more inclusive workplace and community. By embracing these strategies, we can foster an environment where everyone feels valued, respected, and empowered to bring their whole selves to work.

- Addressing bias in hiring and promotion processes is vital to ensure fairness and equal opportunities for all individuals. We delve into practical approaches, drawing on personal stories and research, to challenge and overcome bias and create more inclusive evaluation criteria. By actively addressing and dismantling systemic barriers, we can create an inclusive workplace that recognizes and values diverse perspectives and promotes individuals based on a comprehensive range of factors beyond merit.

- Responding to microaggressions and stereotypes requires both awareness and assertiveness. We can dismantle stereotypes, combat bias, and create a more respectful and inclusive work environment by fostering open dialogue and promoting education.

- Navigating discrimination from superiors can be daunting, but asserting our rights and advocating for fair treatment is essential. We offer practical strategies for confronting discrimination, seeking support, and fostering respectful conversations with superiors. By amplifying our voices and holding leaders accountable, we can contribute to a workplace culture that values and respects all individuals.

- Advocating for systemic change is a collective effort to challenge and dismantle institutionalized biases and barriers. We explore actionable steps and highlight the power of collective action in creating more equitable systems and structures. Through inspiring stories and research, we emphasize the importance of advocating for policy changes, inclusive practices, and a culture of respect and equity.

By embracing courageous conversations and taking action, we can foster a more inclusive, equitable, and empowering work environment where individuals are seen, heard, and valued.

This chapter guides individuals and leaders committed to driving positive change and building workplaces and communities that celebrate diversity, dismantle biases, and promote a sense of belonging for all.

Systemic Barriers in Hiring and Promotion

When it comes to bias in hiring and promotion, there are several systemic barriers to be aware of. These barriers can perpetuate inequality and hinder the progress of underrepresented individuals.

Some additional systemic barriers to consider include the following:

1. ***Lack of diverse representation in decision-making positions***: When those responsible for hiring and promotion decisions lack diversity, it can perpetuate unconscious bias and hinder equitable opportunities.

2. ***Culture fit as a requirement***: Often, hiring and promotion decisions are based on subjective judgments of "fit," which can unintentionally favor individuals who share similar backgrounds or characteristics with the decision-makers. In hiring and promotion decisions, it's essential to focus on "culture add" and "value add" instead of relying on culture "fit." This approach ensures that individuals with diverse perspectives and unique values are recognized and valued for the positive contributions they bring to the organization's culture and overall success.

3. ***Lack of inclusive recruitment and advertising practices***: Biased language, limited outreach to diverse candidate pools, or

exclusive networks can lead to a lack of diversity in applicant pools, limiting the opportunities for underrepresented individuals.

4. ***Bias in evaluation criteria:*** Traditional evaluation criteria may inadvertently favor certain groups and overlook the skills and experiences of underrepresented individuals. It's important to critically examine and revise these criteria to ensure fairness and inclusivity.

5. ***Limited access to mentorship and sponsorship:*** Underrepresented individuals often face challenges in accessing mentors and sponsors who can support their professional growth and advocate for their advancement within organizations.

6. ***Unconscious bias in interview and assessment processes:*** Unconscious biases can influence decision-making during interviews and assessments, leading to unequal evaluations and selection outcomes.

7. ***Pay inequity and wage gaps:*** Systemic biases can result in pay disparities, where individuals from marginalized groups may be paid less for equal work compared to their counterparts.

8. ***Lack of transparency in promotion processes:*** A lack of clear guidelines and transparency in promotion processes can create ambiguity and subjective decision-making, leaving room for bias and favoritism.

Addressing these systemic barriers requires a comprehensive approach that involves challenging biases, implementing inclusive policies and practices, and fostering a culture of diversity and inclusion. By proactively addressing these barriers, organizations can create a more equitable and inclusive environment for hiring and promoting talent.

Addressing Bias in Hiring and Promotion Processes

Through my anti-racism and intercultural work, I've had meaningful interactions in webinars, workshops, and consulting sessions, where I've heard firsthand accounts, like Sarah's, revealing the challenges highly qualified candidates face due to bias in the hiring process. These encounters are a powerful reminder of the ongoing imperative to confront biases and foster inclusive environments, ensuring everyone has an equal opportunity to flourish and succeed.

Sarah is a highly accomplished professional who applied for a senior management position at a medium-sized manufacturing company. Sarah's credentials were impeccable, with a proven track record of exceptional skills, extensive experience, and a long list of impressive achievements.

Throughout the interview process, Sarah couldn't help but notice subtle signs of bias that seemed to be working against her. Despite her stellar qualifications, she found herself facing a level of scrutiny and skepticism. Her responses were dissected more rigorously, and she was subjected to veiled microaggressions disguised as seemingly innocent inquiries about her personal life and commitments.

The experience was disheartening for Sarah. She knew she had the expertise, the experience, and the drive to excel in the role. Yet, despite her bright qualifications, she was not offered the position. It was a moment that highlighted the reality of bias and discrimination that still persist in our workplaces.

Sarah's story is just one example of the bias that many individuals face when seeking employment or promotion opportunities. These biases, whether conscious or unconscious, can lead to the exclusion of talented individuals from accessing career advancement and opportunities for growth. Her story is a reminder of the challenges that talented individuals from marginalized groups face in their professional journeys. It underscores the importance of creating inclusive hiring and promotion processes where qualifications are evaluated fairly and without bias.

By sharing Sarah's experience, we shed light on the need for courageous conversations about bias and discrimination in the workplace. Through these conversations, we can bring about meaningful change, fostering environments where everyone has an equal opportunity to thrive and contribute their unique talents.

A Harvard Business Review (Gino & Wilmuth, 2015) research reveals that unconscious biases significantly influence hiring decisions. These biases can be based on various factors such as race, gender, age, and socio-economic background. Such biases perpetuate inequality and limit the potential for innovation and diversity within organizations.

The impact of bias in hiring and promotion processes goes beyond the individual level and affects overall business outcomes. According to a study conducted by McKinsey & Company (Hunt et al., 2018), companies with more diverse workforces outperform their peers in terms of financial performance. The study found that gender-diverse companies were 21% more likely to experience above-average profitability, while ethnically diverse companies were 33% more likely to achieve the same.

Additionally, a report by the Center for Talent Innovation (2013) highlighted that organizations with diverse leadership teams were more likely to be innovative and make better decisions, leading to improved business performance and competitive advantage.

Integrating Diversity, Equity and Inclusion (DEI) in Talent Management

Talent management is a complex domain encompassing various facets that deserve an in-depth exploration. While a comprehensive examination of talent management would warrant a book on its own, I will specifically address the vital aspect of DEI integration in attracting, developing, and retaining talent. This chapter of the book will emphasize the significance of integrating DEI in hiring and recruitment, demonstrating how it impacts the organization's ability to foster a diverse, inclusive, and thriving workforce.

One key aspect of integration is establishing diverse hiring panels. These panels consist of individuals from diverse backgrounds and experiences who can provide unique perspectives and challenge unconscious biases. By involving a diverse group of decision-makers, organizations can minimize the influence of individual biases and promote fair evaluation of candidates.

In addition to diverse hiring panels, organizations can integrate diversity, equity and inclusion training into the development programs of hiring managers and interviewers. This training raises awareness about unconscious biases, helps individuals recognize their biases, and provides them with the tools and strategies to make unbiased decisions. Organizations can ensure fair and inclusive hiring practices by equipping individuals with the knowledge and skills to navigate biases.

Integrating diversity and inclusion also involves implementing structured interview processes. These processes utilize standardized job-related questions and are asked consistently by all candidates. Believe it or not, some organizations still do not use this!

By focusing on objective criteria and evaluating candidates based on their skills and qualifications, organizations minimize the impact of subjective biases and create a level playing field for all applicants.

Furthermore, organizations can review and refine their job descriptions and qualifications to ensure they are inclusive and not inadvertently exclude underrepresented candidates. By using inclusive language and considering alternative qualifications or experiences, organizations can attract a more diverse pool of applicants and provide equal opportunities for all.

Creating Fair Evaluation Criteria

It is essential to create fair and unbiased evaluation criteria to address bias in hiring and promotion processes. This involves identifying and challenging biases at each stage of the process, from job postings and resume screening to interviews and final selection.

One effective strategy is to implement blind resume screening, where identifying information such as name, gender, and race is removed from resumes. This helps to ensure that candidates are evaluated based on their qualifications and experiences rather than preconceived notions or stereotypes.

In addition, as mentioned earlier, establishing diverse interview panels and incorporating structured interview questions can help address bias. A diverse panel of interviewers brings different perspectives and reduces the likelihood of bias in the evaluation process. Structured interview questions ensure consistency and fairness in assessing candidates, focusing on their qualifications and job-related competencies.

Furthermore, when considering promotion decisions, a comprehensive range of factors beyond merit can be considered. When creating an evaluation criteria that is fair, consider incorporating the following:

1. *Merit and Performance:* While merit is still a relevant factor, it should be considered alongside other factors to provide a holistic assessment of an individual's abilities, skills, and achievements. Evaluating an employee's performance, including their accomplishments, contributions to the organization, and their potential for growth, can provide a more well-rounded perspective.
2. *Competencies and Skills:* Assessing the competencies and skills relevant to the position being considered for promotion is important. This includes both technical skills and soft skills such as leadership, communication, collaboration, adaptability, and problem-solving abilities. Recognizing a diverse set of skills helps identify candidates who can bring unique strengths to the promoted role.
3. *Growth and Potential:* Considering an employee's growth trajectory and potential for development is crucial. Assessing their willingness to learn, take on new challenges,

and their capacity for growth helps identify individuals who have the potential to succeed in higher-level positions, even if they haven't fully demonstrated it yet.

4. *Leadership Abilities:* Evaluating an individual's leadership abilities, including their ability to motivate and inspire others, foster a positive work environment, and effectively manage teams, is important for positions with managerial or supervisory responsibilities.

5. *Diversity and Inclusion:* Promoting diversity and inclusion within the organization can be a factor in promotion decisions. Recognizing individuals who have actively contributed to fostering an inclusive work environment, promoting diversity initiatives, and demonstrating an understanding of different perspectives can be considered alongside other factors.

6. *Continuous Learning and Adaptability*: Assessing an employee's commitment to continuous learning, their ability to adapt to changing circumstances, and their openness to new ideas and approaches is important in a rapidly evolving work environment.

7. *Ethical and Professional Conduct:* Considering an employee's ethical conduct, professionalism, and adherence to organizational values and standards can be important when making promotion decisions, as it reflects their alignment with the organization's culture and values.

One of my consulting clients, Shannon, was a Director of IT in a growing tech company. Shannon was committed to creating a more diverse and inclusive team that would drive innovation and foster a culture of belonging. Recognizing the importance of inclusive hiring practices, she sought my guidance to navigate the complexities of building a diverse team. Together, we developed a comprehensive strategy encompassing every stage of the hiring process, from job postings to final selection.

Shannon wanted her team to seek out candidates from underrepresented backgrounds actively and ensured that the job postings used inclusive language and appealed to a diverse pool of applicants. We worked on refining the job descriptions to remove any unnecessary requirements that might create barriers for underrepresented candidates.

To address biases in the screening and interview process, we implemented blind resume screening. This helped to eliminate unconscious biases by removing personally identifiable information from resumes, allowing candidates to be evaluated solely on their qualifications and experiences.

Shannon and her team adopted a structured and standardized approach during the interview stage. We developed a set of diverse interview panels comprising individuals from various backgrounds and perspectives. This ensured that candidates were assessed by a diverse group of evaluators, reducing the influence of individual biases and promoting fair and objective evaluations.

Through training and workshops, I provided Shannon and her team with the tools and knowledge to recognize and mitigate unconscious biases. They learned to ask behavior-based questions and focus on candidates' skills and qualifications rather than making assumptions based on their backgrounds. They looked at the value-add and culture-add factors of each candidate.

Shannon's commitment to inclusive hiring practices paid off. With a more diverse team, the company experienced a noticeable shift in its dynamics. Diverse perspectives sparked innovation and creativity, resulting in a more robust problem-solving approach and enhanced collaboration. Employees felt a greater sense of belonging and engagement, increasing productivity and retention.

This success story is a testament to the transformative power of inclusive hiring practices. By embracing diversity, an equitable and inclusive process, and challenging biases, Shannon created a team that reflected its diverse customers and harnessed the unique strengths and talents of individuals from different backgrounds. Through our collaborative efforts, Shannon's company became a role model for inclusive practices, inspiring other organizations to build diverse and inclusive teams.

Addressing bias in hiring and promotion processes is not only the responsibility of individuals experiencing bias but also the duty of organizations and leaders. By creating fair evaluation criteria, integrating diversity, equity, and inclusion in the talent management process, and challenging unconscious biases, organizations can unlock the full potential of their talent pool and foster a more inclusive and diverse workforce. Through these collective efforts, we can dismantle the barriers of bias and create a more equitable workplace.

Amplifying Your Voice: Navigating Biased Hiring and Promotion Practices

An Employee's Journey of Empowerment

People would often approach me with curious expressions, seeking guidance on navigating challenging situations they faced at work. Among the recurring questions was one that touched upon a deeply personal experience – speaking up when confronted with biased hiring and promotion practices.

As I listened to their stories, I empathized with their frustrations and fears, for I had once walked in their shoes. It reminded me of a time when I grappled with my professional worth, questioning whether my achievements would ever be recognized.

One day, a young woman, Nadya, approached me hesitantly after one of my workshops. Her eyes revealed vulnerability and determination as she shared her struggle with biased hiring practices. Despite her exceptional qualifications and unwavering dedication, she felt overlooked and undervalued in her workplace.

"I want to speak up," Nadya confided, *"but I fear the consequences. I don't want to jeopardize my career."*

Her words resonated with me, and I knew I had to offer guidance that would empower her to reclaim her voice. With a reassuring smile, I leaned in and began to share my journey of overcoming similar hurdles.

"Nadya," I said, *"you are not alone in this battle. Many of us have faced the same challenges. But remember, speaking up is not a sign of*

weakness; it is an act of strength. Your experiences and talents deserve to be recognized, and you have the right to advocate for yourself."

We talked about the power of storytelling – how sharing our experiences could help create awareness and inspire change and the **S.P.E.A.K.U.P. Model** as her tool. I urged Nadya to document her accomplishments, highlighting her impact on projects and teams and to use those stories as evidence of her value to the organization.

"Your voice can be a catalyst for positive change," I emphasized, *"and you never know who else might be silently facing the same biases. By speaking up, you can pave the way for a more equitable workplace for everyone."*

As our conversation continued, I could see a transformation unfolding within Nadya. The uncertainty that once clouded her eyes was gradually replaced by a newfound resolve. Armed with fresh perspectives and strategies, she felt empowered to take the next steps in her journey.

Weeks later, Nadya reached out to share the remarkable turn of events after our last meeting. Although the position she had hoped for was offered to another candidate, the courageous conversation she initiated opened up an entirely new level of support from her manager. Recognizing her dedication and potential, the manager offered Nadya tailored learning and development opportunities to enhance her leadership skills further.

Through her tenacity, Nadya challenged the biases she had faced. She paved the way for her personal growth and advancement within the organization. The conversation sparked a ripple effect beyond her immediate goal, creating an environment where her contributions were now valued and nurtured.

As we celebrated her achievements, it became clear that speaking up had become a catalyst for positive change Nadya's journey highlighted the transformative power of courageous conversations, where even in the face of initial setbacks, new doors opened, and support emerged to fuel her journey toward success.

This experience served as a poignant reminder of the impact that one brave voice can have. In embracing her worth and advocating for herself, Nadya grew as an individual and contributed to reshaping the workplace into a more inclusive and empowering space for all. It exemplified the essence of the **S.P.E.A.K.U.P. Model** – empowering individuals to assert their voices, challenge biases, and forge a path toward a brighter, more equitable future, one courageous conversation at a time.

As more individuals sought my counsel, I knew that this was a journey we were undertaking together – a collective movement toward a more inclusive and just world, *one courageous conversation at a time.*

An Opportunity for Leaders

Nadya's experience serves as a powerful reminder of the transformative potential that courageous conversations hold. While her manager responded with support and tailored opportunities for growth, not every organization is as receptive.

Suppose they want to create a safe and inclusive work environment. In that case, leaders must recognize the significance of providing a safe space for their employees to speak up about their biases and challenges. As employees muster the courage to address these issues, it presents leaders with an opportunity to practice empathy, actively listen, and take proactive steps toward creating a more inclusive and equitable environment.

Leaders who embrace courageous conversations empower their employees and foster a culture of trust, transparency, and growth. On the other hand, organizations that dismiss or ignore these conversations risk losing valuable talent and potential. The failure to address bias and inequity can lead to disengagement, dissatisfaction, and even attrition among employees who feel unheard and undervalued.

When guiding leaders, I often emphasize to leaders the importance of listening to their employees' experiences and perspectives. By demonstrating genuine interest and support, leaders can pave the way for positive change, driving individual and organizational growth. The courage displayed by employees who initiate these conversations should serve as an eye-opener for leaders, prompting them to reflect on the impact of their responses and fostering an environment where every voice is heard and valued.

At the heart of it all, courageous conversations are not just about addressing biases; they are about building bridges, dismantling barriers, and shaping a workplace that thrives on diversity and inclusivity. In amplifying these voices, leaders can unlock the true potential of their organization and lay the foundation for a brighter and more inclusive future.

A Leader's Inspiring Journey: Empowering Global Leadership with Inclusivity

Amidst the challenges posed by the pandemic, an unexpected opportunity arose when I was invited to facilitate an online workshop for global business leaders. During one of these virtual sessions, I had the privilege of meeting Betty, a dynamic and insightful global leader from a multinational corporation.

Betty's thoughtful contributions and astute observations caught my attention as our workshop delved into the intricacies of diversity, equity, and inclusion. Her curiosity and genuine interest in driving positive change within her organization shone brightly. I could sense her determination to lead with compassion and empathy.

Following the workshop, Betty connected with me for a one-on-one conversation, eager to explore how she could navigate the complexities of addressing bias in hiring and promotion within her global team. Betty shared her concerns about the lack of diversity in leadership roles and her strong belief in the untapped potential of individuals from underrepresented backgrounds.

In our collaborative discussions, Betty revealed that she had encountered resistance from some of her colleagues when she attempted to initiate conversations about diversity and inclusion. However, she remained steadfast in her conviction and was determined to create a culture where everyone felt valued and heard.

I recognized Betty's unwavering commitment and introduced her to the SPEAK UP Model, which offered a structured approach to engaging in courageous conversations. We focused on building Betty's self-assurance and empathetic listening skills, allowing her to connect with her team members on a deeper level.

Through role-playing exercises, Betty practiced articulating her concerns with clarity and assertiveness, gaining the confidence to address biases and foster an inclusive environment. She embraced the concept of "culture add" and "value add," together, we developed strategies to attract and retain diverse talents that would enrich her team's collective experience.

As a global leader, Betty knew the importance of understanding diverse perspectives across cultures and regions. Together, we explored cultural nuances and context-specific approaches to promote inclusivity within her multinational team.

Over time, Betty began to see positive shifts within her organization. She ignited a culture of continuous learning and growth by engaging her team in open discussions about bias and inclusion. Her team members felt empowered to bring their authentic selves to work, knowing their voices were valued and respected.

Betty's fearless dedication to fostering diversity and inclusion reverberated throughout the organization, inspiring other leaders to follow suit. She initiated a series of training and development programs to equip her team with the tools to address bias and create a more inclusive workplace.

As her coach, I was proud to witness Betty's transformational journey. Her tireless efforts and unwavering commitment profoundly impacted the organization, leading to increased employee engagement, heightened innovation, and a stronger sense of belonging among team members.

Betty's story serves as a testament to the ripple effect of courageous leadership. Through her willingness to embrace the discomfort of addressing bias and championing diversity, she ignited a wave of positive change that transcended borders and cultures.

Betty's exemplary dedication to creating an inclusive and equitable workplace stands as a beacon of hope and inspiration in the ever-evolving global leadership landscape. Her journey demonstrates that when leaders like Betty use their voice and influence for good, they can pave the way for a brighter, more inclusive future – *one courageous conversation at a time.*

Practical Actions: If you are the recipient of biased hiring and promotion

- *Build confidence*: Recognize your worth and capabilities. Develop self-assurance in your skills and qualifications. This will strengthen your resolve to address bias and advocate for yourself.
- *Document your achievements*: Keep a record of your accomplishments, contributions, and positive feedback. This documentation can prove your qualifications and help challenge any biased decisions.
- *Seek support:* Reach out to mentors, allies, or employee resource groups within your organization. Share your concerns and experiences and seek guidance on how to navigate the situation effectively.
- *Engage in self-advocacy*: Have open and honest conversations with your supervisors or H.R. representatives. Clearly articulate your

career aspirations and desire for equitable treatment and opportunities. Share specific examples of how your skills and qualifications align with available positions.

- **Request feedback:** Ask for constructive feedback from supervisors or decision-makers regarding your performance and potential areas for growth. Use this feedback to demonstrate your commitment to professional development and advancement.
- **S.P.E.A.K.U.P.**

The Airport Incident: "Are you sure you should be lining up in this lane?"

As an immigrant, I have personally encountered the weight of microaggressions most of the time related to my race and gender, and its impact on one's sense of belonging and self-worth cannot be underestimated.

The seemingly innocuous comments I have faced serve as poignant reminders of the biases and stereotypes that persist in society. Statements like *"You speak good English," "You're an impressive person for someone from your background,"* or *"You're so articulate and assertive for a Filipino woman"* have been directed toward me on multiple occasions.

Although they may be intended as compliments, they contribute to the harmful narrative that individuals who look or sound different are somehow lesser or don't fit into mainstream society.

These comments undermine my accomplishments and perpetuate the notion that my worth as an individual is intrinsically tied to my immigrant status or cultural background. They inadvertently imply that my successes are unexpected or exceptional solely because of my differences rather than recognizing my abilities and efforts on their own merits.

In November of 2022, my mother passed away. I had the responsibility to arrange her funeral so my husband and I had to do an emergency trip to fly back home.

At the airport, I faced another distressing incident of microaggression. We lined up at the Air Canada priority check-in counter, rightfully so, as we are an Aeroplan Elite Status member. However, my experience took an upsetting turn when an Air Canada staff member approached me.

The staff said, *"This is the priority lane."* I politely assured him I knew I was in the correct lane. Despite my response, he asked, *"Are you sure you should be lining up in this lane?"* The sting of his words hit me hard, and I could feel the blood rushing to my face. It was yet another reminder of the biases some people hold, assuming that I, as a person of my background and color, wouldn't belong in the priority check-in lane.

Summoning my composure, I swiftly retrieved my Aeroplan Status Card from the luggage handle of my carry-on bag. I presented it to him, hoping to silence any further doubts. I longed to have a constructive conversation with him about the implications of his comment, but my frustration had to wait. The lady at the check-in counter called for my attention, drawing me away from the situation before it could escalate.

Experiences like this weigh heavily on the soul, leaving me frustrated and disheartened. In times of vulnerability, such microaggressions seem to inflict deeper wounds.

Such microaggressions constantly remind me of being perceived as an incompetent outsider, making it challenging to fully embrace my identity and feel a genuine sense of belonging. They serve as subtle reminders of the persistent biases that continue to shape the experiences of immigrants and people from diverse backgrounds. I believe it is essential to raise awareness about such incidents, as they contribute to broader conversations about discrimination and encourage change.

All individuals must recognize the impact of their words and actively challenge the assumptions and stereotypes ingrained in our society. By fostering a culture of respect, understanding, and inclusivity, we can create an environment where individuals are valued for their talents, experiences, and unique contributions rather than judged based on preconceived notions or limited by harmful stereotypes.

Here are some common examples of racial and gender microaggressions and why these comments are hurtful and perpetuate biases and stereotypes.

- *"You're an impressive leader for someone from your background."*
  - Implying that her background might typically hinder leadership abilities rather than recognizing her leadership skills on their own merits.
- *"You're so articulate and assertive for a woman!"*
  - Suggesting that it's unexpected for a woman, especially a woman of color, to possess strong communication and leadership skills.
- *"Are you sure you're up for this leadership position?"*

- o Questioning her competence and qualifications implies that she might not be capable of handling the role's responsibilities.
- *"You're lucky to have been given this opportunity to lead."*
- o Undermining her achievements by suggesting that her leadership role is a result of luck or affirmative action rather than recognizing her skills and hard work.
- *"You should be more approachable and less intimidating as a leader."*
- o Reinforcing stereotypes that women of color in leadership should conform to certain societal expectations of being warm and nurturing rather than displaying strength and assertiveness.
- *"You're so emotional; you need to be more rational in your decisions."*
- o Stereotyping her emotions as a negative characteristic implies that she can't make sound decisions based on reason.
- *"Your accent might be a barrier to effective communication with the team."*
- o Associating her accent with incompetence, despite her abilities and qualifications as a leader.
- *"We need someone who can better relate to the team culturally."*
- o Assuming that her cultural background inherently prevents her from connecting with her team effectively rather than focusing on her leadership skills.

Triggers or hot buttons that may indicate a microaggression:

1. **Cultural Stereotypes:** Comments or actions that perpetuate stereotypes about a person's race, ethnicity, religion, gender, or other identities.

2. **Assumptions and Generalizations:** Making assumptions about someone based on their appearance, background, or identity without knowing them personally.

3. **Exoticization or Tokenization:** Reducing a person to a stereotype or token representative of their culture or identity.

4. **Microinvalidations:** Dismissing or trivializing someone's experiences of discrimination, often with phrases like "You're just being sensitive" or "It's not a big deal."

5. **Racial or Gender-Based Jokes:** Jokes that target a person's race, gender, or identity, even if they are intended as harmless humor.

6. **Underestimating or Diminishing Accomplishments:** Dismissing a person's achievements or success based on assumptions about their background or identity.

7. **Invisible Identity Negation:** Ignoring or denying a person's identity, experiences, or heritage, such as saying, "You don't look [insert ethnicity/race]."

8. **Language and Pronouns:** Misusing someone's preferred pronouns or using inappropriate language to refer to their identity.

9. **Exclusion or Marginalization:** Leaving someone out of discussions, activities, or opportunities based on their identity or background.
10. **Micro assaults:** Intentional and explicit actions or comments that belittle or demean someone based on their identity.

It is important to remember that microaggressions are often subtle and unintentional, but their impact can be hurtful and perpetuate bias. Recognizing these triggers can help individuals become more aware of potential microaggressions and foster a more inclusive and respectful environment.

The topic of microaggression is of utmost importance, deserving its own dedicated focus. To delve deeper into this significant issue, I recommend exploring the wealth of available resources that provide valuable insights and understanding.

Here are some recommended books on the topic:
1. *"Microaggressions in Everyday Life: Race, Gender, and Sexual Orientation"* by Derald Wing Sue

2. *"Microaggressions and Marginality: Manifestation, Dynamics, and Impact"* edited by Derald Wing Sue
3. *"So You Want to Talk About Race"* by Ijeoma Oluo

Dealing with microaggressions, biases, and discrimination necessitates courageous conversations. To navigate these conversations effectively, consider employing the **S.P.E.A.K.U.P. Model** you learned from this book as a valuable tool to frame your responses. This model can empower you to address such situations with clarity and sensitivity.

However, taking it a step further, I highly encourage you, and if you are in a leadership position, to have your team engage in skill-building workshops that equip them with the tools to effectively handle microaggressions. By participating in these workshops, individuals can gain awareness, learn valuable conversational skills in a safe space, and discover how to heal from the impacts of these experiences.

At The Inclusion Journey Consulting, we offer Courageous Conversation workshops designed to facilitate awareness and foster the growth of essential conversational abilities. These workshops provide a safe and supportive environment for individuals to share their experiences, learn from one another, and develop strategies for effectively responding to microaggressions. Through these workshops, we aim to create a workplace culture that nurtures empathy, understanding, and inclusivity.

Responding to Microaggressions and Stereotypes
The R.E.S.P.E.C.T. Conversation Tool

Imagine a bridge that stands tall, connecting us through respectful dialogue, while empowering us to address microaggressions with grace and assertiveness.

In addition to the **S.P.EA.K.U.P. Model,** let's explore another tool that offers strategies for responding assertively and constructively to microaggressions.

I call this the **R.E.S.P.E.C.T. Conversation Tool** (Figure 5)**,** a conversation tool designed to navigate microaggressions effectively and promote understanding.

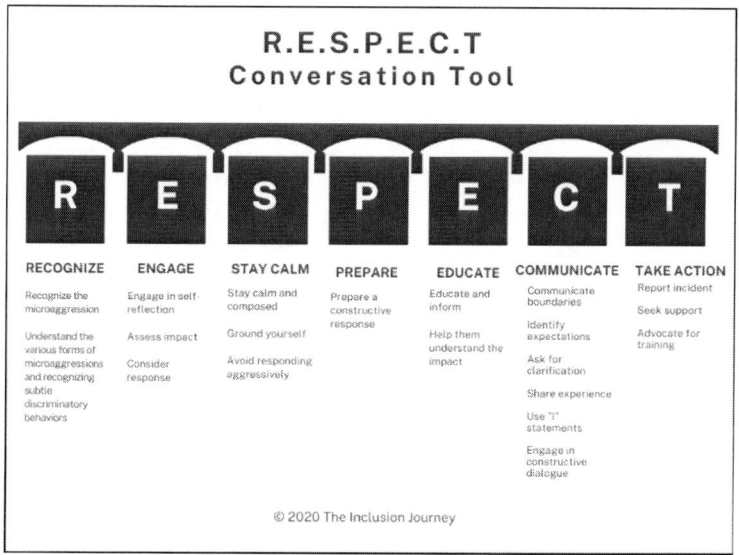

Figure 5: **R.E.S.P.E.C.T. Conversation Tool**

Let's explore further what these pillars are:

R: Recognize the Microaggression: Develop the ability to identify microaggressions when they occur. This involves understanding the different forms of microaggressions and recognizing subtle discriminatory behaviors.

E: Engage in Self-Reflection: Take a moment to reflect on your own feelings and reactions to the microaggression. Assess the impact it has on you and consider how you want to respond.

S: Stay Calm and Composed: Maintain your composure and stay calm during the interaction. Take deep breaths, ground yourself, and avoid responding impulsively or aggressively. This allows you to approach the situation with a clear mind and assertiveness.

P: Prepare a Constructive Response: Plan and prepare your response to the microaggression. Choose language that is assertive, clear, and respectful. Focus on expressing your feelings and thoughts in a non-confrontational manner.

E: Educate and Inform: Use the opportunity to educate the person about microaggressions and stereotypes. Explain how such comments can be hurtful and perpetuate bias. Help them understand the impact of their words on individuals from marginalized communities.

C: Communicate your Boundaries:

o Clearly communicate your boundaries and expectations. Let the person know what acceptable and respectful behavior is. Articulate how you would like to be treated and emphasize the importance of mutual respect. Let the person know that such remarks are not acceptable and create an unwelcoming environment.

o Ask for Clarification: If you are unsure about the intent behind a comment, consider asking for clarification in a non-confrontational manner. This allows the person to reflect on their words and provides a chance for meaningful dialogue.

o Share Personal Experience: If you feel comfortable, share your personal experience to illustrate the impact of microaggressions and stereotypes. Personal stories can be powerful in promoting empathy and understanding.

- Use "I" Statements: Frame your response using "I" statements to convey your feelings and experiences. For example, "I felt hurt when you made that comment because it perpetuates harmful stereotypes."
- Engage in Constructive Dialogue: Encourage open dialogue by inviting the person to discuss their perspective. Be patient and actively listen to their thoughts but be assertive in challenging biased beliefs.
- Redirect the Conversation: If the person becomes defensive or unresponsive, consider redirecting the conversation to focus on the broader issue of discrimination and the importance of fostering inclusivity.

   T: Take Action: Take appropriate action to address the microaggression and discrimination.

- Report the Incident: If the microaggression occurs in a professional or institutional setting, consider reporting the incident to relevant authorities (HR) or supervisors. Many organizations have policies against discrimination and can address such issues appropriately.
- Seek Support: Reach out to supportive colleagues, friends, or community members to share your experience and seek advice. Having a support network can help you navigate these challenging situations.

○ Advocate for Training: Encourage your workplace or community to provide training on diversity, inclusion, and unconscious bias. These workshops can help raise awareness and foster a more respectful and inclusive environment.

The **R.E.S.P.E.C.T. Conversation Tool** serves as a valuable framework for effectively responding to microaggressions. Remember, it's important to approach these situations with assertiveness, empathy, and a commitment to promoting a culture of respect and inclusivity. By using this Tool, you can navigate microaggressions in a constructive manner, contributing to positive change and fostering a more inclusive environment for everyone.

Dealing with Discrimination from Supervisors

Discrimination in the workplace, especially from those in positions of power, can profoundly impact an individual's well-being and professional growth. Discrimination is an issue that hits close to home for some of us. I personally witnessed and experienced the profound impact it can have on one's well-being and professional growth. It is disheartening to see individuals in positions of power use that power to perpetuate discrimination and inequality.

There were several instances where companies faced significant financial losses due to discrimination lawsuits filed by employees. One notable example is the case of Texaco Inc., a major American oil company which faced a racial discrimination lawsuit in the mid-1990s. In 1996, Texaco settled the lawsuit for $176 million, one of the largest settlements at the time, due to allegations of a racially hostile work environment and discriminatory practices.

Another prominent case is the class-action lawsuit against retail giant Walmart. In 2001, a gender discrimination lawsuit was filed against Walmart on behalf of approximately 1.5 million female employees. The case, known as Dukes v. Walmart Inc., alleged systemic gender discrimination in pay and promotion practices. Although the Supreme Court ultimately dismissed the class-action status of the lawsuit, it drew significant attention to issues of gender discrimination in the workplace.

And the list grows longer.

As of 2020, companies facing workplace discrimination, harassment, and retaliation lawsuits in 2020:

- Amazon:
    - Lawsuits accused racially biased hiring practices and COVID-19 safety measures.
    - Discrimination against a pregnant transgender man.
    - Claims of harassment and retaliation against a transgender man and two Black employees.
- Bloomberg LP:
    - Lawsuits alleged aiding and abetting sexual harassment by Charlie Rose and racial and gender bias in pay and promotion practices.
- The Chan Zuckerberg Initiative (CZI):
    - Sued by an ex-employee who claimed Black employees were underpaid, undervalued, and marginalized.
- Disney:
    - Joined by multiple additional women in a lawsuit over gender-based pay discrimination.
- Facebook:
    - Subject of a federal complaint alleging racial discrimination against Black employees and candidates.

- Fox News:
    - Lawsuit accusing ex-host Ed Henry of sexual assault and hosts Tucker

Carlson, Sean Hannity, Howard Kurtz, and Gianno Caldwell of harassment.

- Goldman Sachs:
  - Lawsuit claimed the company covered up sexual misconduct by a top lawyer and retaliated against an employee who spoke publicly about it.
- Google:
  - Lawsuit expanded to include 10,800 additional female employees over gender pay disparities.
- Hearst:
  - Sued by an ex-executive at Esquire magazine for gender and age discrimination.
- Johnson & Johnson:
  - Sued by an ex-executive claiming sexist, harassing, and demeaning behavior by male coworkers.
- Marriott:
  - Sued by a Black ex-employee for racial discrimination and retaliation.
- McDonald's:
  - Facing racial discrimination lawsuits from Black franchisees and a sexual harassment class-action lawsuit.

- Morgan Stanley:
  - Sued by its first diversity officer for racial discrimination and retaliation against

efforts to promote diversity and inclusion.

- The NCAA:
    - Sued by HBCU athletes claiming academic performance policies are biased against their schools.
- Oracle:
    - Expanded gender pay disparities lawsuit to include 4,000 current and former employees.
- Pinterest:
    - Settled a gender discrimination lawsuit with a former executive and facing another lawsuit from shareholders over alleged racial and gender discrimination.
- Uber:
    - Sued by a former driver claiming racial bias in the five-star rating system.
- Warner Bros.:
    - Sued by a former executive alleging gender discrimination and harassment from senior male executives.
- WeWork:
    - Sued by former employees for discrimination, harassment, and intimidating behavior, including bringing weapons to work.

The growing number of workplace discrimination, harassment, and retaliation lawsuits underscores several key aspects:

- **Awareness:** The prevalence of discrimination lawsuits indicates that workplace discrimination is still a significant issue. While progress has been made in raising awareness about diversity and inclusion, there is still much work to be done to create truly inclusive and equitable workplaces.
- **Fear of Speaking Up:** The fact that employees resort to lawsuits to address discrimination suggests that many may fear retaliation or lack confidence in their company's internal reporting mechanisms. This highlights the need for fostering a safe and supportive environment where employees feel comfortable speaking up without fear of consequences.
- **Limited Impact of One-Off Training:** One-off or isolated training sessions may not be enough to create lasting change in organizational culture. To address workplace discrimination effectively, training should be ongoing, reinforced, and integrated into various aspects of the organization's operations.
- **Need for Comprehensive Training:** Comprehensive training programs that cover topics like unconscious bias, cultural competence, bystander intervention, and inclusive leadership are essential. Such training can help employees recognize and address discriminatory behaviors and promote a culture of respect and understanding.

- **Role of Leadership:** The involvement and commitment of leadership in promoting diversity and inclusion are crucial. Leaders should champion these efforts and actively participate in training programs to set an example for the rest of the organization.
- **Holistic Approach:** Addressing workplace discrimination requires a holistic approach that encompasses not only training but also policy changes, transparent reporting mechanisms, diversity in hiring, and continuous evaluation of progress.
- **Empowerment and Support:** Employees need to feel empowered to report discriminatory incidents and believe that their concerns will be taken seriously. Companies must ensure that support systems are in place to protect whistleblowers and address grievances effectively.
- **Long-Term Strategy:** Organizations should view diversity and inclusion efforts as a long-term strategic goal rather than a checkbox exercise. By investing in sustained and comprehensive training, they can foster a culture that values and embraces diversity.
- **Accountability:** Holding individuals and the organization accountable for their actions and behaviors related to discrimination is essential. This includes addressing issues promptly, taking corrective action, and implementing systemic changes to prevent future incidents.

- **Learning and Growth:** Companies must view workplace discrimination cases as opportunities for learning and growth. Each case can serve as a catalyst for introspection, identifying areas of improvement, and implementing positive changes.

The increasing number of discrimination lawsuits emphasizes the ongoing need for organizations to prioritize diversity, inclusion, and equity through comprehensive and continuous training, fostering open communication, and promoting a culture where everyone feels valued and respected.

Practical Actions

For Individuals:

1. **Educate Yourself:** Take the initiative to educate yourself about various forms of discrimination, microaggressions, and harassment. Understanding these concepts can help you recognize them in your workplace.

2. **Speak Up and Support:** If you witness discrimination, microaggressions, or harassment, speak up and support the affected individual. Encourage open conversations and offer empathy and understanding. Use the

framework, model and tools shared in this book to make the courageous conversation.

3.	**Report Incidents**: If you experience or witness discriminatory behavior, promptly report it to your company's HR department or appropriate authorities. Ensure you follow the organization's established reporting procedures.

4.	**Challenge Biases:** Be aware of your own biases and work to challenge and overcome them. Engage in introspection and actively seek opportunities to be more inclusive and open-minded.

5.	**Be Respectful:** Treat all colleagues with respect and dignity, regardless of their background, gender, race, or other characteristics. Promote a positive and inclusive work environment.

6.	**Practice Active Listening**: Listen attentively to others' experiences and concerns, especially if they have faced discrimination or harassment. Validate their feelings and experiences.

7.	**Be an Ally:** Advocate for diversity and inclusion initiatives. Support underrepresented colleagues and be an ally in their fight against discrimination.

For Leaders and Organizations (yes, I have a longer list for leaders and organizations)

1. **Create Clear Policies:** Establish comprehensive anti-discrimination and anti-harassment policies that outline expected behavior and consequences for violations. Communicate these policies to all employees.

2. **Provide Training:** Offer regular training on diversity, unconscious bias, cultural competency and inclusive leadership for all employees. Ensure that employees understand the importance of creating an inclusive workplace.

3. **Promote Diversity in Leadership:** Strive for diversity in leadership positions to create a more inclusive organizational culture. Encourage diverse representation at all levels of the company.

4. **Ensure Accountability:** Hold individuals accountable for discriminatory behavior, regardless of their position within the organization. Treat all reported incidents seriously and conduct impartial investigations.

5. **Establish Reporting Mechanisms**: Implement confidential and accessible reporting channels for employees to report discrimination, microaggressions, and harassment without fear of retaliation.

6. **Support Targets of Discrimination**: Provide support and resources for employees who experience discrimination, harassment, or microaggressions. Offer counseling or access to employee assistance programs.

7. **Promote an Inclusive Culture**: Foster a culture of respect and inclusion by celebrating diversity and recognizing the value that diverse perspectives bring to the organization.

8. **Regularly Evaluate Progress**: Continuously assess the effectiveness of diversity, equity and inclusion initiatives. Use metrics to measure progress and identify areas for improvement.

9. **Conduct Workplace Climate Surveys**: Periodically conduct surveys to gauge employees' perceptions of the workplace climate. Use the feedback to inform targeted interventions.

10. **Lead by Example**: Leaders should exemplify inclusive behaviors, demonstrate cultural competence, and actively participate in diversity and inclusion efforts.

11. **Create Safe Spaces**: Leaders should strive to establish safe spaces where employees feel comfortable speaking up about instances of discrimination. This may involve implementing anonymous reporting systems, organizing town hall meetings or open forums, and encouraging honest and open dialogue. By providing a platform for employees to share their experiences, concerns, and suggestions, leaders can gain insights and take appropriate action.

12. **Supporting and Empowering Employees**: This includes providing guidance, resources, and mentorship opportunities to help

them navigate challenging situations. Leaders encourage employees to document instances of discrimination and offer support in seeking redress or filing complaints when necessary.

13. **Collaborate with HR and Management**: Leaders work closely with HR and management to develop and enforce policies that promote fairness and address discrimination. This collaboration may involve reviewing hiring and promotion processes, ensuring diversity in decision-making panels, and implementing regular diversity and inclusion training for all employees. By partnering with key stakeholders, leaders can create a more equitable workplace culture.

14. **Engage in Courageous Conversations:** Leaders recognize the importance of engaging in courageous conversations with superiors or colleagues who exhibit discriminatory behavior. These conversations are approached with empathy and assertiveness, sharing the impact of their actions and advocating for fair treatment. By engaging in these conversations, leaders can raise awareness, challenge biases, and foster positive change.

By taking these practical actions, individuals and organizations can contribute to creating a more equitable, inclusive, and respectful workplace, where all employees feel valued, supported, and empowered.

Advocating For Systemic Change

I remember working with a client, a leader in the healthcare industry, who was passionate about creating positive change within their organization. They had personally experienced the effects of systemic biases and witnessed the barriers that marginalized individuals faced in their workplace. Inspired by their journey, they wanted to advocate for systemic change and improve the overall system to foster a more inclusive and equitable environment.

This client recognized that addressing individual incidents of discrimination was not enough. They understood the importance of challenging the underlying systems and structures perpetuating inequities. They wanted to create lasting change that would benefit themselves, their colleagues, and future generations.

Driven by their determination, this client embarked on a journey to become an advocate for systemic change. They sought to educate themselves and others about the existing systemic biases and barriers. Through conversations, research, and engaging with diverse perspectives, they deepened their understanding of the complexities of systemic issues.

Armed with knowledge and a passion for change, this client began actively amplifying the voices of marginalized individuals within their organization. They created spaces for open dialogue and facilitated discussions on anti-racism, cultural competence, unconscious bias, diversity, equity, and inclusion. By elevating these voices and sharing their stories, they shed light on the experiences of those who had been marginalized or overlooked.

This client also recognized the importance of collaborative partnerships in effecting change. They connected with like-minded individuals, organizations, and advocacy groups to form alliances and pool resources. Together, they championed inclusive policies, lobbied for legislative reforms, and advocated for fair and equitable practices within their organization.

Through their commitment to continuous learning and growth, this client challenged their biases and assumptions. They actively sought feedback and embraced discomfort while navigating conversations around privilege, power dynamics, and systemic biases. This self-reflection allowed them to evolve as advocates and approach their work with empathy and understanding.

This client's journey exemplifies the power of individuals who are determined to make a difference. Their dedication to advocating for systemic change transformed their workplace and inspired others to join their cause. By taking action and leveraging their influence, this client became a catalyst for positive change, creating an environment where everyone felt valued, respected, and empowered.

In advocating for systemic change, we recognize that it requires a collective effort to challenge and dismantle institutionalized biases and barriers. It goes beyond addressing individual incidents of discrimination and focuses on addressing the root causes and structural inequalities that perpetuate inequitable systems.

To become effective advocates and agents of change, we can employ various strategies within the workplace and the broader community.

Practical Actions

Practical Actions when Advocating for Systemic Change:

1. **Education and Awareness:** Building awareness and understanding systemic issues is a critical first step. By educating ourselves and others about the historical context, social inequalities, and systemic biases, we can better articulate the need for change and engage in meaningful conversations.

2. **Amplify Marginalized Voices:** Advocating for systemic change involves actively amplifying the voices of marginalized individuals and communities. By providing platforms and opportunities for them to share their experiences and perspectives, we can bring attention to the systemic inequities they face and work towards dismantling those barriers.

3. **Collaborative Partnerships:** Creating meaningful change often requires collaboration and partnership. By joining forces with like-minded individuals, community organizations, and advocacy groups, we can leverage collective resources and influence to drive systemic change. Together, we can advocate for policy reforms, challenge discriminatory practices, and promote inclusive policies within our organizations and society.

4. **Engage in Policy Advocacy**: Advocating for systemic change also involves engaging in policy advocacy. This may include supporting or advocating for legislation that promotes diversity, equity, and inclusion. By participating

in public policy discussions, contacting elected representatives, and supporting initiatives that aim to address systemic inequalities, we can contribute to creating a more equitable society.

5. **Fostering Inclusive Workplace Practices**: Advocating for systemic change within the workplace involves promoting inclusive practices and policies. This includes ensuring fair hiring and promotion processes, providing equal opportunities for professional development, and creating a supportive and inclusive work culture. By advocating for diversity and inclusion initiatives, we can drive systemic change at the organizational level.

6. **Continuous Learning and Growth:** Systemic change requires ongoing learning, self-reflection, and growth. It is important to stay informed about current social issues, engage in conversations about privilege and power dynamics, and challenge our biases and assumptions. By committing to continuous learning and growth, we can advocate for systemic change more effectively.

Intent alone falls short;
it is through
acknowledging
the far-reaching impact of
our words and actions
that we wield
the power to
uplift or diminish others.

Maria Drueco

Chapter 7
Prioritizing Your Well-Being

"Self-care is not a luxury but a sacred duty we owe to ourselves. For it is from this place of nourishment that we can better serve and support those around us."
- *Maria N. Drueco*

When we prioritize self-care, we replenish our inner reservoirs, enhancing our mental clarity, enabling us to be more compassionate, patient, and present in our interactions with others.

These are the building blocks that enable us to pursue our ambitions, achieve personal growth, and foster stronger connections with others. We become better equipped to handle life's challenges, face biases and stereotypes, and address difficult conversations with courage and grace. We become more resilient, purposeful, and fulfilled, capable of positively impacting ourselves and the world around us.

On the other hand, neglecting self-care can lead to an imbalance in our lives, hindering our ability to meet higher-level needs. Like a structure without a stable foundation, we may find ourselves vulnerable to burnout, stress, and emotional exhaustion, preventing us from fully realizing our potential and reaching the pinnacle of self-actualization.

In essence, embracing self-care is not an act of self-indulgence but a critical investment in our well-being, a fundamental necessity for maintaining our overall health and vitality. Only when we care for ourselves can we authentically care for others.

Self-Care Strategies for Building Resilience

Resilience, I've come to realize, is firmly rooted in the practice of self-care. As a member of marginalized groups, particularly as an immigrant, I've faced unique challenges in my professional and personal life. I know firsthand how being resilient helped me in navigating these obstacles. Let me share a story that highlights the transformative power of resilience for individuals like us.

I recall the early days of our move to Canada, brimming with anticipation yet accompanied by a sense of unease. Lifestyle change, lack of extended family and support network, cultural adjustments, and the perpetual feeling of being an outsider presented daunting obstacles. It was challenging, and at times, it felt overwhelming. In the face of this new reality, I quickly grasped the importance of self-care as a cornerstone for navigating this journey with resilience.

After all, in the midst of it all, I realized that prioritizing self-care was not just about me; it was about ensuring that I could be there for my husband and children. By taking care of myself, I could support them, guide them through the uncertainties of our new life while also instilling in my children the value of resilience and self-empowerment.

Through consistent self-care, I noticed a transformation within myself. Resilience became my strength. I became more self-aware and attuned to my needs. I learned to navigate challenges with greater adaptability and emotional balance. Through this journey of self-discovery and growth, I learned that nurturing my well-being was not selfish but vital for both myself and those I loved.

The Combined Power of Growth Mindset + Resilience: Turn Challenges into Opportunities

Growth mindset and resilience are psychological concepts described as attitudes or beliefs rather than specific traits or behaviors. These attitudes/ beliefs influence how we approach and respond to challenges and setbacks. They are not fixed traits but rather flexible beliefs that can be developed and strengthened over time through self-awareness, practice, and intentional effort.

Here's how we can define them:

Growth Mindset:

A growth mindset is a belief that abilities and intelligence can be developed through effort, learning, and perseverance. Individuals with a growth mindset believe they can improve their skills and abilities over time through dedication and hard work. They see challenges as opportunities for growth and are not discouraged by setbacks or failures. Instead, they view them as learning experiences and use them to adapt and improve.

Resilience:

Resilience is the capacity to bounce back from adversity, challenges, and setbacks. It involves the ability to cope with difficult situations, recover from setbacks, and maintain a positive outlook despite facing obstacles. Resilient individuals can better navigate life's challenges, maintain emotional well-being, and adapt to changes.

By adopting a growth mindset and cultivating resilience, individuals can enhance their ability to overcome obstacles, learn from experiences, and achieve personal growth and success.

Navigating My Journey with Growth Mindset and Resilience

As Carol Dweck, the renowned psychologist, and researcher on mindset, emphasizes, challenges are not roadblocks but opportunities for greatness. This rings particularly true for individuals like me, who face unique obstacles in our pursuit of success. Navigating biases, stereotypes, and systemic barriers has been daunting. Still, embracing a growth mindset and resilience has allowed me to transform these challenges into opportunities for greatness; as stepping stones to personal and professional growth.

I have learned from setbacks, adapted to changing circumstances, and recognized that my unique perspectives and experiences are assets, not hindrances. With each hurdle I overcome, I become more determined, more confident, and more capable of creating meaningful change in my life and the lives of others. I have learned to challenge preconceptions and rewrite my own narrative.

Individuals like me, who identify as a Person of Color, underrepresented, immigrant, and those who belong to other marginalized groups should expect that the journey toward success can be marked by encounters with biased perceptions, limited opportunities, and feelings of exclusion. It is easy to feel disheartened by these obstacles but find the strength to face them head-on through resilience.

Practical Actions

Practical self-care strategies that can help us build resilience and nurture overall well-being

1.   **Mindfulness Practices:** Mindfulness is a powerful tool for self-care and resilience. Taking moments throughout the day to practice mindfulness helps us stay present, reduce stress, and enhance our overall well-being. Whether through meditation, deep breathing exercises, or simply paying attention to the present moment, mindfulness can provide a sense of calm and clarity in our lives.

Incorporating mindfulness into our self-care routine can have profound benefits for our well-being and resilience.

Here are some resources that can guide and support us in cultivating mindfulness practices:

- "The Miracle of Mindfulness: An Introduction to the Practice of Meditation" by Thich Nhat Hanh: This classic book introduces us to the transformative power of mindfulness through practical guidance and insightful teachings. Thich Nhat Hanh offers simple techniques that can be applied in everyday life to cultivate mindfulness and reduce stress.

- "Wherever You Go, There You Are: Mindfulness Meditation in Everyday Life" by Jon Kabat-Zinn: Jon Kabat-Zinn, a renowned mindfulness teacher, shares practical advice and exercises to incorporate mindfulness into our daily lives. This book explores how mindfulness can enhance our well-being, reduce anxiety, and promote a greater sense of presence and connection.

- Headspace App: The Headspace app offers a variety of guided mindfulness meditations and exercises for beginners and experienced practitioners alike. With its user-friendly interface and diverse range of meditation topics, the app provides a convenient way to integrate mindfulness into our daily routine.

- Calm App: The Calm app provides a wide range of mindfulness and meditation resources, including guided meditations, sleep stories, and breathing exercises. It offers tailored programs for different needs, such as stress reduction, improved focus, and better sleep, making it a comprehensive tool for practicing mindfulness.

- Mindful.org: Mindful.org is a website dedicated to mindfulness and its applications in various aspects of life. It features articles, guided practices, and resources that can deepen our understanding and practice of mindfulness. Exploring the articles and resources on Mindful.org can provide valuable insights and inspiration for incorporating mindfulness into our self-care routine.

Mindfulness is a personal journey, and it's important to find the resources and techniques that resonate with you. Experiment with different approaches and resources to discover what works best for you in cultivating mindfulness and integrating it into your self-care practices.

2.   **Self-Compassion Exercises**: Self-compassion is an essential component of self-care. It involves treating ourselves with kindness, understanding, and acceptance, especially during challenging times. Engaging in self-compassion exercises, such as positive self-talk, self-acceptance, and self-forgiveness, can help us build resilience and foster a nurturing relationship with ourselves.

Cultivating Self-Compassion Guide
To support you in cultivating self-compassion as part of your self-care routine, I have prepared a set of questions to cultivate self-compassion.

These questions will guide you through exercises and reflections to enhance your self-compassion practices.

1. *Self-Reflection:* Take a moment to reflect on your current level of self-compassion.
   - Are there areas in your life where you may need to offer yourself more kindness and understanding?
2. *Positive Self-Talk*: Explore positive affirmations and self-talk that can counteract negative self-judgment and cultivate a more compassionate inner dialogue.
   - How can you reframe self-critical thoughts with kinder and more supportive language?
3. *Self-Acceptance:* Engage in exercises to foster self-acceptance and embrace your inherent worth and value.
   - Take the time to acknowledge and appreciate your strengths, talents, and unique qualities.
4. *Self-Forgiveness:* Forgiving ourselves for past mistakes or perceived shortcomings is essential to self-compassion.
   - Can you identify areas where you may be holding onto self-blame?
   - How can you cultivate forgiveness and compassion for yourself?

5. ***Integration and Application:*** Consider how to integrate self-compassion into your daily life.
   - What self-compassion practices can you incorporate into your self-care routine?
   - Create an action plan and set intentions for nurturing yourself with kindness and understanding.

Using this **Cultivating Self-Compassion Guide**, you can deepen your understanding of self-compassion and develop practical strategies to nurture yourself with kindness and compassion.

Self-compassion is a journey, so be patient and gentle with yourself as you embrace this transformative practice.

3. **Activities that Bring Joy and Relaxation:** Engaging in activities that bring us joy and relaxation is crucial for our well-being. These activities can vary for each person, but they should be things that truly bring us happiness and help us unwind. It could be practicing a hobby, spending time in nature, reading a book, listening to music, or engaging in creative pursuits. We recharge our energy and nourish our souls by dedicating time to activities that bring us joy.

One activity that brought me immense joy was taking long walks in nature. I would find happiness and solace in the peacefulness of the surrounding trees, the gentle breeze on my face, and the soothing sounds of birds chirping. During these walks, I allowed myself to let go of worries and be present in the beauty of nature.

Engaging in activities that bring joy and relaxation is a form of self-care and a way to replenish our energy and foster a sense of well-being. It's a reminder that amidst the busyness of life, we deserve moments of pure joy and tranquility.

Finding activities that bring you joy and relaxation is a personal journey. Take the time to explore what truly makes your heart sing and incorporate those activities into your routine. Your well-being deserves it.

4. **The Transformative Power of Travel:** Travel is a remarkable self-care tool that allows us to explore new cultures, gain fresh perspectives, and rejuvenate our overall well-being.

The transformative power of travel lies not only in the physical act of going to a new place but also in the internal journey it triggers. It opens our minds, broadens our perspectives, and allows us to understand ourselves and the world around us. It reminds us that there is so much more to life than our immediate surroundings and routines. Traveling lets us step outside our comfort zones, broaden our horizons, and create lasting memories. Whether a short getaway or an immersive travel experience, traveling helps us break from routine, reduce stress, and find inspiration in new environments.

I have always been fascinated by the transformative power of travel.

My first trip out of the country was an eye-opener for me. As I immersed myself in the new environment and culture, I was exposed to different ways of life, traditions, and perspectives. I stepped out of my comfort zone, trying new foods, exploring unfamiliar neighborhoods, and conversing with locals. Each experience brought a sense of exhilaration and a renewed appreciation for the diversity and richness of our world.

Traveling also provided a much-needed break from the monotony of routine. It offered a reprieve from the pressures of work and responsibilities, allowing me to recharge and refocus. Being in new surroundings ignited my creativity and inspired me to see the world through a different lens.

During my travels, I always discovered that being in a new environment awakened my senses and sparked a sense of curiosity within me. As I immersed myself in different cultures, interacting with people from diverse backgrounds, I began to understand the significance of this unique perspective—a traveler's mindset.

A Traveler's Mindset

A traveler's mindset goes beyond being a mere spectator in a foreign land; it is an active and open approach to learning about different cultures, traditions, and beliefs.

As I engaged with locals, embraced their customs, and celebrated their festivals, I became more culturally aware and appreciative of our world's rich tapestry of diversity.

This journey of exploration and discovery naturally cultivated cultural competency—a profound understanding and appreciation for cultures beyond my own. It is a journey of learning and growth, where one gains insights into the values, norms, and practices that shape various societies.

Embracing a traveler's mindset has allowed me to navigate the complexities of multicultural interactions with sensitivity and empathy. I have learned to approach cultural differences with curiosity rather than judgment, recognizing that these differences enrich our lives and broaden our horizons.

Incorporating these self-care strategies into our daily lives requires commitment and intention. It's important to prioritize self-care and make it a non-negotiable part of our routine. Start by identifying the self-care practices that resonate most with you and find ways to integrate them into your daily schedule. Create a self-care plan that includes specific activities and allocate dedicated time for them.

Self-care is not selfish; it's an essential investment in our well-being and resilience. By taking care of ourselves, we are better equipped to navigate the challenges and uncertainties that come our way. Let's start doing these practical self-care approaches and prioritize our well-being, knowing that we deserve it.

Financial Empowerment
Financial well-being is an essential aspect of overall wellness, and knowing practical

strategies to manage finances can empower us to achieve a more balanced and secure life.

There is a deep connection between financial well-being and mental health. Financial stress can impact your overall sense of well-being, and by nurturing your financial health, you can cultivate greater peace of mind and resilience in the face of adversity.

Before I share some practical tips, let me take you on a journey that many immigrants and individuals from marginalized groups embark upon—a journey filled with dreams, aspirations, and the pursuit of a better life.

For immigrants like me and our families, the decision to immigrate was not one made lightly. It came with significant financial costs, sacrifices, and uncertainties. We had to consider visa fees, legal expenses, and the expenses of uprooting our lives. It was an investment in our future, in the hopes of providing our children with greater opportunities and a brighter tomorrow.

Once we arrived, the reality of the situation set in. Finding work was no easy feat. Despite our qualifications and experiences, the job market was competitive and unfamiliar. We faced the challenge of establishing ourselves in a new society, navigating communication barriers, and adapting to a different culture.

The cost of living in our new country was higher than what we were accustomed to, adding to the financial strain. We had to learn to budget carefully and prioritize our expenses, all while trying to build a foundation for our family's future.

At times, the uncertainty of not having a guaranteed job and the financial burden felt overwhelming. It was a test of our resilience, determination, and resourcefulness. But through it all, we held on to the belief that this journey was an investment in our dreams and aspirations.

Why am I sharing this?

I'm sharing this journey because it highlights the unique financial challenges immigrants and individuals from marginalized groups encounter. We often face the challenge of wage and pay inequity, which adds a layer of complexity to our financial situation.

Studies have shown that the gender pay gap in Canada is exacerbated for racialized women, Indigenous women, and women with disabilities. These disparities impact our financial security and can have ripple effects on our mental health and overall well-being.

Numerous studies and reports have shed light on the wage disparities faced by immigrants, especially women, in Canada and the US. Notable studies include:

- Statistics Canada Report (2021): A study by Statistics Canada revealed that immigrants in Canada, particularly those who arrived within the past five years, encounter wage disadvantages compared to non-immigrants. Despite having similar education and work experience, recent immigrants tend to earn less than their non-immigrant counterparts.

- Canadian Women's Foundation (2022): Women in Canada earn significantly less than men, with women making approximately $0.87 for every dollar earned by men. This disparity exists across various industries and occupations, reflecting a persistent and widespread issue. The gender pay gap is particularly pronounced for women from marginalized communities, such as Indigenous women, racialized women, and women with disabilities. These women face even more significant wage disparities than non-marginalized groups, highlighting the intersectionality of the issue. The gender pay gap not only impacts women's current earnings but also has long-term consequences for their retirement savings and financial security.

- National Bureau of Economic Research (NBER) Study (2019): A research paper published by the NBER revealed that immigrants in the US, regardless of gender, earn lower wages compared to non-immigrants. The study attributed this wage disparity to various factors, including language barriers, recognition of foreign qualifications, and discrimination.

- US Bureau of Labor Statistics Data (2021): The US Bureau of Labor Statistics reported that foreign-born workers, including women immigrants, tend to earn lower wages than their native-born counterparts. This disparity is more pronounced for recent immigrants and individuals with limited English proficiency.

These data underscore the urgent need for continued efforts to address the gender pay gap and achieve more significant equity and fairness in the workplace.

Aside from wage disparities, other significant financial challenges and disparities faced by members of marginalized groups can impact their overall well-being and financial security.

Some of the issues they may encounter include:

1. **Limited Access to Opportunities:** Immigrants and individuals from marginalized groups may have limited access to career advancement opportunities, promotions, and leadership positions, hindering income growth.
2. **Discrimination and Bias:** Discrimination and bias in hiring and promotions can lead to fewer job opportunities and unequal pay for individuals based on their ethnicity, gender, or immigrant status.
3. **Lack of Financial Literacy:** Many immigrants and individuals from marginalized groups may not have access to financial education and resources, leading to challenges in managing their finances effectively.
4. **Cultural Barriers:** Cultural norms and practices can influence financial decision-making. Some individuals may face pressure to financially support extended family members, impacting their ability to save or invest.
5. **Limited Access to Financial Services:** New immigrants and marginalized groups may face barriers to accessing traditional financial services such as banking, credit, and loans, making it challenging to build credit and access financial support.
6. **Systemic Inequalities:** Systemic barriers and societal inequalities can affect wealth accumulation and financial opportunities for immigrants and marginalized groups.
7. **Mental Health Impact:** Financial stress and insecurity can lead to increased mental health

challenges, affecting overall well-being and productivity.

Practical Actions for Individuals:
- **Budget:** Create a detailed budget to track your income and expenses. Be mindful of your spending habits and identify areas where you can save money.
- **Save:** Establish an emergency savings fund to provide a safety net for unexpected expenses. Consider automating your savings to make it easier to set money aside regularly.
- **Invest:** Educate yourself about investment options that align with your financial goals. Start investing early to take advantage of compound interest and long-term growth.
- **Build Financial Resilience:** Focus on building resilience to financial setbacks by diversifying your income streams and continuously upgrading your skills to remain competitive in the job market.
- **Engage in Financial Planning:** Seek the help of a financial planner/ advisor to develop a comprehensive financial plan that outlines your short-term and long-term goals, such as buying a home, paying off debt, or saving for retirement. They can provide personalized advice based on your unique circumstances.
- **Mindfulness and Stress Reduction:** Recognize the impact of financial stress on your

mental health and well-being. Engage in mindfulness practices and stress-reducing activities to maintain balance.

- **Community Support:** Connect with community organizations that offer financial education and support. These resources can provide valuable insights and opportunities for networking.
- **Advocacy and Allyship:** Advocate for equitable financial opportunities and policies within your community and workplace. Allyship with others facing similar challenges can foster mutual support and empowerment.
- **Continuous Learning:** Stay informed about financial matters and seek opportunities for financial education and skill-building workshops.

Incorporating these strategies into your financial planning and decision-making can empower you to navigate financial challenges effectively and work towards achieving your financial goals with confidence and resilience.

Supporting Financial Empowerment of Marginalized Groups

Organizations embracing equitable hiring practices and fair compensation hold the power to be catalysts for the financial empowerment of marginalized groups. To address the systemic issues perpetuating inequity and financial disempowerment, visionary leaders must spearhead comprehensive and proactive efforts.

Practical Actions for Leaders:

- *Addressing Pay Gap/Inequity in Your Organization:* Take proactive steps to identify and rectify any wage disparities. Conduct regular pay equity analyses to ensure that employees are compensated fairly based on their skills, qualifications, and contributions, regardless of their gender, race, or ethnicity. Implementing transparent pay policies can promote a culture of fairness and inclusivity.

- *Implementing Skills-Based Hiring:* Move away from traditional hiring practices that may perpetuate bias and stereotypes. Embrace skills-based hiring, where candidates are assessed based on their abilities and potential to excel in the role rather than relying solely on past experiences or credentials. This approach increase access to opportunities and helps diversify the talent pool and create a more inclusive work environment.

- *Provide Financial Education Programs:* Recognize the link between financial well-being and mental health. Offer financial education programs and resources as part of your employee well-being initiatives. These programs can equip employees with the knowledge and tools to manage their finances effectively, reduce financial stress, and foster overall well-being.

- **_Cultivate Inclusive Leadership_**: Foster a culture of inclusive leadership within your organization. Encourage leaders to be aware of their biases and actively work to create a supportive and inclusive environment. By promoting open dialogue and actively listening to the perspectives of diverse team members, leaders can cultivate an inclusive team culture that values and respects individual contributions.

- **_Establish Mentorship and Sponsorship Programs:_** Create mentorship and sponsorship programs that offer support and guidance to underrepresented employees. These programs can help individuals from marginalized communities navigate their career paths, access opportunities for growth and advancement, and foster a sense of belonging within the organization.

- **_Diversify Leadership and Decision-Making:_** Ensure that your leadership team and decision-making bodies reflect the diversity of your workforce and customer base. By promoting representation and diversity at the highest levels of your organization, you signal a commitment to equity and inclusivity, which can positively impact the company's culture and bottom line.

- **_Encourage Courageous Conversations_**: Foster an environment where employees feel safe and encouraged to have courageous conversations about bias, stereotypes, and inequities. Provide training and resources to help employees develop communication and conflict-resolution skills, promoting open and constructive discussions that lead to positive change.

By taking these practical actions, leaders can play a pivotal role in fostering financial empowerment for marginalized groups. Equitable hiring practices ensure equal access to job opportunities, closing the wage gap uplifts individuals economically, and fair compensation supports upward mobility and reduces wealth inequality. Moreover, inclusive practices enhance employee engagement and retention. At the societal level, financially empowered individuals contribute to economic growth and break generational cycles of poverty.

Advocating For Oneself: Courageous Conversation Tips When Asking for a Pay Raise

Asking for a raise is a natural and crucial aspect of career growth, reflecting our value, contributions, and accomplishments within our organization. The courage to advocate for oneself demonstrates confidence and commitment to achieving our full potential. It empowers us to actively shape our career trajectory and align our compensation with your skills and achievements.

Easier said than done, right?

As with all courageous conversations, asking your manager for a raise can be nerve-wracking! Still, you can increase your chances of success with thoughtful preparation and confidence.

Practical Actions
Here are some tips for approaching this conversation:
- **Research and Preparation**: Before the conversation, gather information about industry salary standards and your specific job role's market value. Be prepared to explain how your contributions and achievements have positively impacted the organization.
- **Choose the Right Timing:** Pick a suitable time to discuss the raise with your manager. Avoid approaching the topic during busy or stressful periods for your manager or the company.
- **Highlight Your Achievements:** Showcase your accomplishments, projects you've successfully led, and any extra responsibilities you've taken on. Be clear about how your efforts have contributed to the team's success.

- **Practice Confidence:** Confidence is key during the conversation. Practice what you want to say beforehand and maintain a calm and composed demeanor.
- **Quantify Your Value:** Use data and specific examples to demonstrate your value to the organization. Highlight any cost savings, revenue generation, or efficiency improvements you've made.
- **Know Your Worth:** Understand your skills, expertise, and the unique value you bring to the team. Believe in the value of your contributions and express it with conviction.
- **Be Open to Discussion:** Be open to negotiating and consider other benefits or opportunities if a raise isn't immediately possible.
- **Stay Positive and Professional:** Maintain a positive and professional attitude throughout the conversation. Avoid sounding entitled or comparing yourself negatively to others.
- **Listen Actively:** Pay attention to your manager's response and be open to feedback. Ask for clarification if needed and show that you value their input.
- **Follow Up:** If the conversation doesn't lead to an immediate raise, inquire about the possibility of a future review and set a timeline for further discussion.

Taking these steps is about recognizing your worth and fostering a workplace culture that values and rewards talent and dedication. Embrace the opportunity to have a courageous conversation with your employer and seize the moment to showcase the value you bring to the table. Approach the conversation with a clear understanding of your worth, backed by evidence of your contributions. Be respectful and professional in your communication.

Build a Supportive Network

Seeking professional support is crucial to maintaining your well-being and fostering personal and professional growth.

Let's talk about the importance of allies, mentors, and supportive networks in our journey. Allies, mentors, and supportive networks are vital in providing guidance, encouragement, and a sense of belonging. Building strong connections with allies and mentors can be a game-changer, providing valuable insights, advice, perspectives, expertise, and opportunities to advance our careers and navigate challenges.

These relationships can offer valuable insights, perspectives, and expertise to help you navigate challenges, make informed decisions, and achieve your goals. Allies are individuals who stand by your side, advocate for your rights, and support you in breaking down barriers. Mentors are experienced professionals who offer guidance, share their wisdom, and help you develop your skills and knowledge. Supportive networks are communities of like-minded individuals who uplift and empower each other through shared experiences and resources.

Let's explore how these supportive relationships can empower us to achieve our goals and reach new heights in our lives.

Allies, Mentors, and Networks

Becoming An Ally: The Power of Advocacy and Action

Being an ally is not a self-proclaimed title; it is a recognition bestowed upon individuals based on their actions and advocacy work. Being an ally has transformative impact on individuals and communities.

I emphasize that true allyship is about actively supporting and advocating for marginalized groups, standing up against injustice, and working towards creating a more inclusive and equitable society. It is not a passive role, but rather an ongoing commitment to learning, growth, and action.

As allies, we understand the importance of acknowledging our power and privilege. Recognizing how our position in society can impact others allows us to use that influence responsibly. When we choose to stand alongside marginalized communities, we demonstrate our commitment to equality, justice, and inclusivity. Our support and advocacy can help break down barriers, challenge stereotypes, and foster environments that celebrate diversity and embrace the unique contributions of every individual.

Through intentional efforts, we can create positive change and make a meaningful difference in the lives of those around us. We can advocate for equitable policies and challenge discriminatory practices by leveraging our influence, resources, and connections. As allies, we have a vital role in leveling the playing field and dismantling systemic barriers. Our actions go beyond mere acknowledgment; they are directed toward creating a more inclusive and fair society where everyone has equal opportunities to thrive and succeed. It's about helping build environments that uplift and empower individuals from all walks of life, ensuring everyone's voice is heard and valued.

Allyship In Action

I want to share a powerful story of allyship in action that exemplifies the transformative impact of Equity, Diversity, and Inclusion (EDI) efforts. This story revolves around Morgan, a remarkable leader and visionary who serves as the manager at the Library. As a consultant engaged in Morgan's EDI work, I have witnessed firsthand the genuine compassion and dedication she brings to her role.

Before her tenure, the Library lacked a strategic policy and direction related to EDI. However, the Library made significant strides under Morgan's leadership and consultation with staff and community partners.

Through collaboration with experts in the field of EDI, she guided the Leadership Team in creating the Library's first EDI policy. This foundational step established accountability and paved the way for ongoing EDI goals, ensuring that the Library's practices are supportive, accessible, and equitable.

Morgan's EDI approach is community-driven, regularly engaging with equity-deserving groups and individuals. She has worked closely with businesses and organizations run by Indigenous, People of Color 2SLGBTQI+ to establish "knowledge groups," host an Indigenous online course, and an anti-racism workshop for the public and professionals, all while ensuring these programs and services are supported by the involved individuals and groups. By actively collaborating with these communities, she has nurtured meaningful partnerships and implemented initiatives that positively impact the lives of many.

As a role model, Morgan embodies EDI principles professionally and personally. From displaying flags of equity-deserving groups in her office to providing opportunities for professional development and actively listening to staff and the public, she exemplifies unwavering support and selflessness for EDI.

Morgan's story is a testament to the power of allyship. It demonstrates that allyship is about acknowledging privilege and actively using it to uplift and empower others. Her courage in fostering courageous conversations and her unwavering support for marginalized communities have made a difference.

Exploring Allyship: A Call to Action for Everyone

When doing workshops on Allyship, I often get this question: is Allyship only for White people? Can a Person of Color be an Ally too?

Absolutely! Let me explain further...

People of Color (POC) can also ally with other marginalized groups.

The traditional definition of allies as individuals who use their power, privilege, and resources to help marginalized communities was developed in the context of dominant groups supporting marginalized groups.

However, the concept of being an ally has evolved to recognize that anyone, regardless of their background, can actively support and advocate for those facing systemic barriers and discrimination. POC and others who may also have power and privilege within specific contexts or situations can stand in solidarity with other marginalized groups and use their unique experiences, perspectives, and resources to create positive change. So, the invitation to Allyship is not just for the White or dominant groups but has expanded to include People of Color.

Being an ally is not solely based on a person's identity or background; it is about taking intentional actions to support and uplift others. People of color can be allies by recognizing their shared struggles with other marginalized communities and working together to dismantle systemic inequity.

Ultimately, Allyship is about unity, empathy, and collective action to create a more inclusive and equitable world for everyone.

Empowered A.L.L.Y.S Framework

A practical roadmap that I teach my workshop participants as a starting point for becoming an effective ally is the **Empowered A.L.L.Y.S Framework** (Figure 6). In this framework, we recognize that being an ally is not simply a label or a passive role but a dynamic process that requires active engagement and commitment. ALLY is a verb, not a noun.

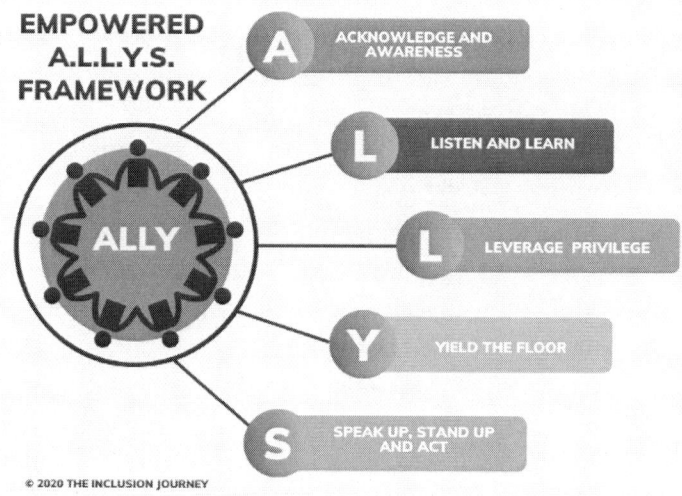

© 2020 THE INCLUSION JOURNEY

Figure 6: **Empowered A.L.L.Y.S. Framework**

Here is an overview of the framework:

- **A - Acknowledge and Awareness:**
  The first step in becoming an empowered ally is raising awareness. It involves educating ourselves about different cultures and the experiences, challenges, and systemic barriers faced by marginalized communities. Through continuous learning and listening, we can develop a deeper understanding of the issues at hand and recognize our own biases and privileges.

- **L - Listen and Learn:**
  As allies, it is crucial to be active listeners and lifelong learners. We must listen to the voices

and stories of those affected by discrimination and inequity, acknowledging their lived experiences and perspectives. By learning from their narratives, we can gain valuable insights that inform our allyship. Be open to constructive feedback and be willing to unlearn and relearn.

- **L - Leverage Privilege:**
Allyship means leveraging our own privilege to amplify the voices of marginalized individuals. It involves using our platform, resources, and influence to create positive change and advocate for equitable opportunities and representation. Stand up against discrimination and challenge biased attitudes or behaviors.
- **Y - Yield the floor:**
Recognize when it's important to step back and let marginalized individuals take the lead. Create opportunities for their voices to be heard and respected. Avoid speaking over or silencing them.
- **S – Speak Up, Stand Up and Act:**
True allyship involves taking proactive steps to combat bias, discrimination, and inequity. It means using our voice and influence to challenge oppressive systems and practices. By actively supporting and advocating for marginalized groups, we become agents of change.
This framework encourages self-reflection, empathy, and taking proactive steps to support marginalized communities.

Allies are like a breath of fresh air, infusing our workplace with positivity, support, and understanding.

Look around, and you'll find these fantastic colleagues, supervisors, and mentors who are ready to stand by us and make positive change happen. So, let's lean on each other, find strength in our collective commitment.

From Adversary to Ally: The Power of Courageous Conversation

It will not always be a walk in the park. In this journey of allyship, courageous conversations hold a critical significance. As we encounter resistance and initial skepticism from those who may not yet understand the importance of diversity and inclusion, we have an opportunity to transform hearts and minds through dialogue.

Rather than reacting with anger or defensiveness, we take the reins of the conversation, steering it towards understanding and growth. We approach these moments with grace and empathy, recognizing that some may need to be educated about the experiences of marginalized communities. With open hearts and minds, we engage in sincere conversations, asking questions, sharing our stories, and fostering empathy. We create a foundation for genuine connections and transformative change by giving others space to express their perspectives.

The power of courageous conversations lies in our ability to move forward together. We become agents of education and advocates for positive change. We build bridges of understanding, compassion, and solidarity as we embrace these interactions.

When we dare to have courageous conversations, we unlock the true potential of allyship.

A Mentor's Gift: Empowering Minds, Transforming Lives

A mentor is an experienced and trusted advisor who provides guidance, support, and knowledge to a less experienced individual (mentee) to help them grow, develop skills, and achieve their goals. A mentor shares their expertise, insights, and personal experiences to offer valuable guidance and perspective.

It's a common misconception to equate mentors and coaches, but they have some important distinctions. While both involve supportive relationships to foster growth, mentoring takes a more comprehensive and long-term approach, concentrating on the mentee's overall personal development. On the other hand, coaching tends to be more targeted, focusing on specific goals and skill enhancement within a specific context.

Mentoring and coaching can be likened to two different lenses through which we view personal and professional growth. Mentoring is like a wide-angle lens, encompassing the broader picture of an individual's development and providing guidance and support across various aspects of their journey.

On the other hand, coaching is akin to a zoom lens, allowing us to focus intensely on specific skills or goals, honing in on the details and fine-tuning them for success.

Both lenses are essential in shaping our path to greatness, offering unique perspectives to enrich our growth.

In a workplace setting, the supervisor or manager often assumes the role of a coach, working closely with employees to enhance their skills, address performance goals, and support their professional growth within the context of their roles. The coaching relationship typically revolves around improving job performance and achieving specific objectives.

On the other hand, mentoring can come from someone who may or may not be part of the same department or organization. It is a more informal and voluntary relationship where the mentor provides guidance, wisdom, and career advice based on their own experiences and knowledge.

Mentors focus on the individual's overall development, helping them navigate their career journey, build confidence, and make informed decisions.

Both coaching and mentoring are valuable tools in personal and professional development, and each lens offers unique perspectives to enrich our growth. Understanding the distinctions between these two forms of support allows us to effectively leverage the power of mentoring and coaching, fostering growth and success in our personal and professional lives.

Why Having a Mentorship Program Matters

Several studies and statistics highlight the benefits of having a mentorship program in retaining employees:

- According to a study by Gartner, employees with mentors are 5 times more likely to be promoted than those who do not have mentors. This illustrates the positive impact of mentorship on career progression and employee growth within the organization.
- A report by Deloitte found that organizations with solid mentorship programs have higher employee engagement and retention rates. Engaged employees are likelier to stay with the company and contribute to its success.
- The Association for Talent Development (ATD) reported that 71% of Fortune 500 companies have formal mentorship programs. These programs have become integral to attracting and retaining top talent in competitive industries.
- A study published in the Journal of Vocational Behavior found that mentorship positively influences job satisfaction and organizational commitment. Satisfied and committed employees are likelier to stay loyal to the company and contribute to its long-term success.
- A survey by Forbes revealed that 94% of employees who received mentorship were more likely to stay with the company for longer than a year. This statistic highlights how mentorship

can create a sense of loyalty and dedication among employees.

- According to another report, 68% of millennials believe having a mentor is essential to their professional growth and job satisfaction. As millennials become a significant portion of the workforce, catering to their development needs through mentorship can be crucial for retention.

These statistics demonstrate the positive impact of mentorship programs on employee retention. By providing guidance, support, and opportunities for growth, mentorship programs can create a sense of belonging, development, and loyalty among employees, leading to higher retention rates and long-term success for organizations.

How Mentorship Transformed my Life, my Career and my Business

Recalling a turning point in my career when my manager approached me with an exciting opportunity. She asked if I would be interested in being part of a mentorship program within our corporate organization. Without hesitation, I eagerly said yes, recognizing the potential for growth and learning that this mentorship could offer me.

Soon after, I was paired with a senior HR leader in the company, someone with a wealth of experience and wisdom to share. Our mentorship journey began, and I quickly realized the profound impact it would have on my personal and professional development. I embarked on this mentoring journey with a sense of excitement and curiosity. I approached my mentorship experience with an open mind and a willingness to learn. From our very first meeting, it was clear that my mentor shared my manager's passion for nurturing talent and fostering growth.

Under my mentor's guidance, I began to navigate challenges and explore new opportunities with a renewed sense of purpose. He generously shared their knowledge, experiences, and insights, helping me gain a broader perspective on my field and the intricacies of professional success. His guidance was not limited to career advice; he also emphasized the importance of personal development and work-life balance.

The support I received from my mentor was invaluable in shaping my professional growth. He provided me with constructive feedback, encouraged me to step outside my comfort zone, and challenged me to set ambitious goals. His mentorship helped me identify my strengths and weaknesses, guiding me towards areas where I could further develop and refine my skills.

Beyond his expertise and guidance, my mentor also became a trusted confidant and advocate. He provided a safe space for me to share my challenges, frustrations, and aspirations. He celebrated my successes and helped me navigate setbacks, offering unwavering support and encouragement throughout my mentorship journey. Through our regular meetings and discussions, my mentor guided me in honing my critical thinking, problem-solving, and consulting skills.

As my corporate career progressed, I decided to venture into the world of travel entrepreneurship. Being an independent travel business owner came with its unique set of challenges and uncertainties. Remembering the transformative power of mentorship, I realized that seeking guidance from someone with an established travel business could be the key to my success.

Through my existing network in the travel business, I set out to find a mentor who had a reputable travel business and shared a passion for empowering others in the industry. After reaching out to a seasoned travel entrepreneur, I nervously asked if he would be open to becoming my mentor. To my delight, he warmly welcomed the idea and agreed to guide me on my entrepreneurial journey.

Having experienced mentorship in my corporate life, I understood how instrumental it could be in my personal and professional growth. However, this time, I witnessed its transformative power in the context of my own business. My mentor offered invaluable advice, shared lessons learned from his experiences, introduced me to travel suppliers I would only have met through him, and helped me confidently navigate the complexities of the travel industry.

Through mentorship, I have gained more than just knowledge and skills; I have found a supportive ally, a confidant, and a source of inspiration. The impact of mentorship extends far beyond the professional and business realm; it has enriched my personal life, fostering resilience and a growth mindset.

From my corporate career to my independent business venture, mentorship has been the guiding light that illuminated my path to success. It taught me the value of seeking guidance, the power of shared wisdom, and the importance of empowering others through mentorship.

Today, I stand as a testament to the profound transformation that mentorship can bring to one's life, and I am eternally grateful for the mentors who have shaped my journey into the empowered individual I am today.

Giving Back: Empowering Others Through Mentorship and Advocacy

After experiencing the transformative power of mentorship in my own life, I felt compelled to pay it forward and make a positive impact on others.

As a volunteer mentor to new immigrants and aspiring travel business owners, this experience only reinforced the challenges I knew they already faced—imposter syndrome, a lack of confidence, and the burden of battling bias, stereotypes, and microaggressions. It felt like listening to a broken record as their stories echoed all too familiar struggles.

Their stories echo a recurring pattern of challenges and resilience. This fueled my determination to help them rediscover their self-worth, gain self-confidence, and empowerment.

These compelling stories of strength and perseverance became the driving force behind my workshops and conversations with leaders. I share these real-life experiences to shed light on the issues of inequity, discrimination, and bias—particularly faced by women, immigrants, and People of Color.

These stories have power and can serve as catalysts for change for leaders, nudging them to confront these systemic challenges head-on and take meaningful action to create inclusive and equitable environments.

I discovered that empowering others was an enriching experience in this journey of giving back. The mentorship relationships I forged allowed me to share knowledge and guidance and uplift and elevate the voices of those who often go unheard. Through mentorship, I have witnessed the ripple effect of positive change, and it has strengthened my conviction that we can collectively create a more just and equitable world.

The Power of Accountability

As a mentee, I quickly realized the importance of developing accountability in this relationship. I needed to take ownership of my growth and actively engage in the mentorship process. I embraced the responsibility of setting goals, seeking feedback, and implementing the advice and insights provided by my mentor. By demonstrating my commitment and dedication to my own development, I made the most of the mentorship experience.

Similarly, as a mentor, I recognized the importance of accountability in fostering a successful mentoring relationship. I was responsible for providing guidance, sharing my experiences, and offering constructive feedback. However, I also encouraged my mentees to take ownership of their growth, set goals, and actively seek opportunities for learning and development. By nurturing a sense of accountability, I aimed to empower my mentees to drive their own success.

Throughout my journey as both a mentee and a mentor, I have come to appreciate the reciprocal nature of the mentorship relationship. It is not solely about the mentor imparting knowledge and guidance; it is a two-way street where both parties benefit from the exchange. As a mentee, I gained valuable insights, support, and guidance that shaped my professional growth. As a mentor, I had the privilege of making a positive impact on the lives of others while also deepening my knowledge and understanding.

Accountability is crucial in ensuring that the mentorship relationship is meaningful and impactful. By holding ourselves accountable as mentees, we maximize the benefits of mentorship and actively contribute to our growth. Likewise, as mentors, being accountable to our mentees allows us to provide the guidance and support they need to thrive.

A successful and transformative mentorship journey requires mutual accountability and commitment. Two-way accountability enhances the effectiveness of the mentorship relationship and ensures that both parties derive maximum value. With accountability, we create an environment of trust, growth, and learning that propels us toward our personal and professional goals. So, whether you are a mentee or a mentor, remember the power of accountability in shaping the success of the mentorship journey.

Creating Meaningful Mentorship Connections: Have a Strategic and Courageous Approach

Practical Actions for Individuals
Approaching a mentor can feel intimidating, but you can create a meaningful connection with a strategic and courageous approach.
Here are some practical guidelines that apply the principles of courageous conversations:

1. **Clarify Your Goals:** Before approaching a potential mentor, reflect on your goals and what you hope to gain from the mentorship relationship. Identify the specific areas in which you seek guidance and support. A clear understanding of your goals will help you articulate your needs when contacting a potential mentor.

2. **Research and Identify Potential Mentors:** Conduct research to identify individuals who align with your goals and have the expertise or experience you seek. Look for mentors with a track record of supporting and guiding others whose values and approaches resonate with you. Professional networks, industry associations, and online platforms can be valuable resources for finding potential mentors.

3. **Craft Your Approach:** Once you have identified a potential mentor, prepare a thoughtful and concise message to initiate the conversation. Start by expressing your admiration for their work or achievements and highlight why you believe they would be a valuable mentor. Share a brief overview of your goals and explain why their guidance would be beneficial to your growth. Be genuine, sincere, and respectful in your approach.

4. **Request a Meeting:** Propose a meeting or conversation to discuss the possibility of mentorship. Offer to meet at a convenient time and location, whether in person or virtually.

Clearly communicate your intentions and desired outcomes for the meeting, ensuring that the potential mentor understands your expectations and the purpose of the discussion.

5. **Demonstrate Your Commitment:** During the conversation, demonstrate your commitment and eagerness to learn and grow. Share your willingness to invest time and effort in the mentorship relationship. Discuss the specific areas in which you hope to gain guidance, and express your openness to feedback and constructive criticism. Show that you value their expertise and are willing to actively engage in the mentorship process.

6. **Be Open to Feedback and Suggestions:** During the meeting, be open to receiving feedback and suggestions from the potential mentor. Listen attentively to their insights and advice, and ask thoughtful questions to deepen your understanding. Show genuine interest in their experiences and perspectives, and demonstrate that you value their expertise.

7. **Discuss Expectations:** Clarify expectations and boundaries to ensure a mutual understanding of the mentorship relationship. Discuss the frequency and format of your interactions, preferred communication channels, and specific topics or focus areas. Establishing clear expectations helps create a solid foundation for the mentorship journey.

8. **Express Gratitude:** At the end of the meeting, express your gratitude for their time

and consideration. Thank them for their willingness to explore the possibility of mentorship and acknowledge the value they bring to the table. Follow up with a personalized thank-you note or email to reinforce your appreciation.

9. **Be Prepared:** There's always a possibility of rejection. The mentor may only be available to take on a mentee at a later time. If this happens, maintain a positive attitude. Ask if they know someone who would be interested in being a mentor. The important thing to remember is not to give up. Continue your search for a suitable mentor who aligns with your goals and values.

Approaching a mentor requires courage and confidence. By trying these guidelines and embracing courageous conversations, you increase the likelihood of establishing a successful mentorship relationship that will support your personal and professional growth.

Practical Actions for Leaders

A mentorship program can be a powerful tool for developing People of Color (POC), supporting their growth, and fostering an equitable and inclusive workplace. Mentorship offers a safe and supportive space for POC to navigate their career journeys, gain valuable insights, and build self-confidence. It also enhances cultural competence among all employees, promoting empathy and understanding across diverse backgrounds.

Practical Actions

Here are some practical actions for leaders to create meaningful mentorship connections within their organizations:

1. ***Establish Clear Objectives****:* Clearly define the objectives and desired outcomes before launching a mentorship program. Identify specific areas where POC may need additional support and focus on fostering an inclusive environment that values diverse perspectives and experiences.

2. ***Provide Training and Resources:*** Offer mentorship training to mentors and mentees to ensure they understand their roles and responsibilities. Provide resources and tools to help mentors effectively guide their mentees, including best practices for cross-cultural communication and understanding unconscious biases.

3. ***Cultivate Inclusive Mentorship Pools:*** Ensure the mentorship pool includes diverse and inclusive representation. Encourage leaders at all levels of the organization to participate as mentors and employees from different backgrounds, experiences, and departments.

4. ***Offer Voluntary Participation:*** Make mentorship programs voluntary to ensure mentors and mentees are genuinely invested in the process. This fosters a supportive and authentic environment where meaningful connections can flourish.
5. ***Promote Mutual Respect and Empathy:*** Encourage mentors to actively listen and show empathy for their mentees' experiences. Foster an open, trusting environment where mentees feel comfortable sharing their challenges and aspirations.
6. ***Set Clear Expectations:*** Facilitate open discussions between mentors and mentees to set clear expectations for the mentorship relationship. Define the frequency of meetings, preferred communication channels, and mutual goals to ensure alignment.
7. ***Create Safe Spaces for Dialogue:*** Organize regular group discussions or forums for mentors and mentees to share their experiences, learn from one another, and build a sense of community and belonging.
8. ***Recognize and Celebrate Success:*** Acknowledge and celebrate the achievements and progress of mentorship pairs. Recognizing these accomplishments reinforces the value of mentorship and encourages continued engagement.

9. *Evaluate and Adjust:* Regularly assess the effectiveness of the mentorship program through feedback from mentors and mentees. Use this information to make necessary adjustments and improve the program's impact.

10. *Lead by Example:* Demonstrate the importance of mentorship by actively participating in the program as a leader. Lead by example, showing a commitment to diversity, equity, and inclusion within the organization.

By implementing these practical actions, leaders can create a mentorship program that supports the development of employees and fosters an inclusive workplace where everyone can thrive.

Unlocking Fresh Perspectives: The Power of Reverse Mentoring

Reverse mentoring is when a younger or less experienced employee mentors a more senior or more experienced colleague. This is also a powerful practice to develop your diverse group of employees and improve inclusion and equity. It is a unique and innovative approach to mentoring that challenges the traditional mentoring dynamic, where more senior, more experienced individuals typically mentor younger or less experienced individuals.

In reverse mentoring, the mentee becomes the mentor, offering insights, knowledge, and perspectives that might not be readily available to the more experienced colleague.

The concept of reverse mentoring gained popularity as technology and digital advancements started playing a more significant role in the workplace. Younger employees, who are often referred to as digital natives, possess a natural familiarity with technology and modern trends, making them valuable mentors for their more senior counterparts. Some DEI-committed companies have successfully implemented reverse mentoring programs to promote diversity, inclusivity, equitable succession planning, and knowledge exchange.

Some notable examples include:
- IBM: IBM has pioneered reverse mentoring programs, pairing younger employees with senior executives to foster cross-generational learning and understanding.
- General Electric (GE): GE is known for its successful reverse mentoring initiatives, where junior employees mentor senior executives, particularly in areas related to technology and digital innovation.
- Procter & Gamble (P&G): P&G has embraced reverse mentoring to bridge the generation gap,

improve communication, and enhance mutual learning among employees of different age groups.

- Microsoft: Microsoft has implemented a "Reverse Mentorship Circle" program, where younger employees mentor senior leaders to provide insights into emerging trends and technologies.
- The Hartford: This insurance company has introduced reverse mentoring programs to enhance diversity and promote intergenerational collaboration within the workplace.
- Unilever: Unilever has implemented reverse mentoring programs to encourage open dialogue and knowledge exchange between senior leaders and younger employees.

Reverse mentoring can benefit both parties involved. This practice can foster a more inclusive and collaborative work environment where knowledge flows in both directions, breaking down hierarchical barriers and encouraging open communication and learning across generations. Reverse mentoring is a powerful tool for promoting continuous learning and fostering a knowledge-sharing culture within organizations. It allows for a unique exchange of knowledge, experiences, and perspectives between employees from different generations and backgrounds, promoting workplace diversity, equity, and inclusion.

For a diverse mix of individuals spanning various age groups, abilities, ethnicities, and genders, reverse mentoring provides an opportunity to share their insights on issues related to diversity, cultural competence, and the experiences of marginalized communities. They can help their more senior colleagues better understand the challenges they face in the workplace and society at large.

On the other hand, your diverse group of more experienced employees can mentor their younger or less experienced colleagues, sharing their wisdom, guidance, and advice on navigating the corporate landscape, breaking barriers, and achieving career success. This knowledge exchange can help the younger diverse group build their confidence, develop their leadership skills, and navigate the challenges of being underrepresented in the workplace.

Reverse mentoring can lead to a more inclusive and supportive work environment. It breaks down stereotypes, fosters empathy, and promotes a culture of mutual respect and understanding. By embracing reverse mentoring, organizations can tap into their employees' diverse perspectives and talents, creating a more equitable and inclusive workplace that benefits everyone involved.

When Reverse Mentorship Program Makes Sense

There are several organizational objectives where reverse mentorship is beneficial. Here are some examples:

- **Diversity and Inclusion Initiatives**: Reverse mentoring is often used in diversity and inclusion programs, especially when fostering greater understanding and empathy between employees from different backgrounds. By encouraging individuals from diverse backgrounds to mentor their more senior colleagues, organizations can create opportunities for open dialogue and greater cultural awareness.
- **Bridging Generational Gaps**: In multi-generational workplaces, reverse mentoring can bridge the gap between older and younger employees. Younger employees can mentor their senior counterparts on technology, social media, and emerging trends. In contrast, more senior employees can offer their experience and insights to help younger employees navigate the professional landscape.

- **Leadership Development:** Reverse mentoring can be used as a tool for leadership development, enabling aspiring leaders to learn from more experienced leaders while also providing senior leaders with fresh perspectives from emerging talent. This approach helps build a leadership pipeline and encourages continuous learning at all levels of the organization.
- **Promoting Learning and Skill Development**: Reverse mentoring can foster skill development and knowledge-sharing between employees with different expertise. For example, an employee with expertise in data analytics can mentor a colleague from a different department to enhance their analytical skills.
- **Building Inclusive Workplace Cultures:** Utilizing reverse mentoring as part of a broader strategy for building inclusive workplace cultures can increase employee engagement, retention, and overall satisfaction. Employees who feel valued for their contributions and experiences are more likely to thrive and contribute to the organization's success.

When Reverse Mentoring Won't Be Suitable
Reverse mentoring may not be suitable in certain situations or organizational contexts.

Here are some scenarios where it may not be the best approach:

- **Resistance to Diversity and Inclusion**: An organization must be genuinely committed to fostering diversity and inclusion; otherwise, implementing reverse mentoring could be perceived as a superficial attempt to appear inclusive without addressing deeper issues.
- **Lack of Openness to Change:** For reverse mentoring to succeed, mentors and mentees must be open to new perspectives and ideas. If either party is resistant to change or unwilling to embrace different viewpoints, the relationship may not be productive.
- **Power Imbalance:** In some cases, there may be a significant power imbalance between the mentor and the mentee, such as when a high-ranking executive mentors a junior employee. This power dynamic could hinder open communication and inhibit the mentee's willingness to share candid feedback.
- **Inadequate Support and Resources:** For reverse mentoring (or any mentoring program, for that matter) to thrive, organizations need to provide sufficient resources, training, and support to both mentors and mentees. The program may struggle to deliver meaningful results if these elements are lacking.
- **Cultural Sensitivity Concerns**: If reverse mentoring is implemented without proper consideration for cultural sensitivity and

awareness, it could inadvertently lead to misunderstandings or reinforce stereotypes.

- **Time Constraints:** For any mentoring relationship to be effective, it requires time and commitment from both parties. If mentors or mentees have overly demanding schedules or conflicting priorities, the relationship may not be sustainable.
- **Unrealistic Expectations:** Organizations may be disappointed if they expect immediate and dramatic changes from a reverse mentoring program. Building trust and fostering meaningful connections takes time and effort.

The above reasons of why reverse mentorship won't work should be addressed first prior to creating this program. It is essential for organizations to carefully assess their specific circumstances and goals before implementing reverse mentoring. Please don't make this just another check-in-the-box exercise.

Other Support Networks

Building a supportive network goes beyond individual connections and encompasses formal structures and resources that organizations can provide.

A supportive network uniquely influences a person's development and well-being. They provide resources, mentorship, emotional support, and access to opportunities.

These supportive networks are beneficial not only for marginalized groups but also for anyone seeking empowerment and growth, as well as organizations aiming to empower their teams. These networks offer opportunities for skill development, mentorship, a sense of belonging, access to new projects, advocacy, and emotional support. By engaging with these networks, we can enhance our personal and professional lives, and organizations can foster an inclusive and supportive work culture that enables their teams to thrive and achieve their full potential.

Let's explore the importance of building a supportive network and the various components that contribute to it. Let's dive into the critical elements of a supportive network:

- **Sponsors:**
  Sponsors are the wind beneath your wings, lifting you higher and farther than you could imagine. They propel your career with their powerful gusts of advocacy, providing you with opportunities and guidance to soar toward success.

They are influential individuals within an organization who advocate for and actively support the career advancement of others. They use their position and influence to provide opportunities, visibility, and guidance to help their protégés succeed. Sponsors can significantly impact an employee's professional growth by providing access to new projects, promotions, and networks. They serve as a source of valuable advice and can help navigate organizational politics. For example, a sponsor may nominate their protégé for leadership development programs or recommend them for high-visibility assignments.

- **Employee Resource Groups (ERGs):** ERGs are voluntary, employee-led groups that provide a sense of community and support for individuals who share common backgrounds, identities, or experiences. ERGs foster inclusivity, drive cultural change, and create a supportive work environment. They offer networking opportunities, mentorship programs, and educational initiatives.

ERGs can significantly impact employees' sense of belonging and engagement within the organization. For example, a Women's ERG may host workshops on leadership development or provide a platform for women to share their experiences and perspectives.

Imagine ERGs as the heartbeat of inclusivity, forming a supportive rhythm that resonates throughout the workplace. Like a tightly-knit community, they create a symphony of understanding, empowerment, and belonging, nurturing each member's unique voice and harmonizing their experiences.

- **Professional Associations and Networking Groups:** These external networks are the bridges that connect you to a world of endless possibilities. They comprise professionals from a specific industry or field who come together to share knowledge, resources, and opportunities. Joining professional associations and networking groups allows individuals to connect with like-minded peers, stay updated on industry trends, and expand their professional network. These networks provide access to mentoring relationships, job postings, and professional development events. For example, a marketing professional may join a digital marketing association to connect with industry experts, attend conferences, and gain insights into emerging marketing strategies.

- **Peer Support Groups:** Peer support groups are the anchors that keep you steady amidst life's storms. They could be individuals facing similar challenges or sharing common goals. These groups provide a safe and supportive space to share experiences, exchange advice, and provide emotional support. Peer support groups can be formal or informal and can be created within an organization or externally. For example, a group of working parents may form a peer support group to share strategies for work-life balance or provide support during challenging times.

Fostering Inclusion through Supportive Networks

Let me share with you the story of a company called TechConnect, a leading technology firm known for its commitment to diversity and inclusion. TechConnect recognized the importance of building supportive networks to foster a thriving workplace environment.

To achieve this, TechConnect established various employee resource groups (ERGs) that catered to its employees' diverse identities and interests. These ERGs provided a platform for employees to connect with one another, share experiences, and advocate for change. One such ERG was the Women in Tech group, which aimed to empower and support women in the male-dominated tech industry.

Employees could access mentorship opportunities, professional development workshops, and networking events through the Women in Tech group. The ERG also collaborated with other ERGs within the company, such as the 2SLGBTQI+ and BIPOC (Black, Indigenous, and People of Color) groups, to create intersectional dialogue and initiatives.

TechConnect understood that these networks not only provided support to individuals but also contributed to the organization's overall success. By fostering an inclusive environment and empowering employees through these networks, the company experienced higher employee engagement, increased retention rates, and a boost in innovation.

The success of TechConnect's approach can be seen in the story of Alex, a software engineer at the company. Alex joined TechConnect as a recent graduate and navigated a predominantly male-dominated industry. Feeling isolated initially, she sought support from the Women in Tech group. Through this network, she connected with a senior mentor who provided guidance, shared valuable insights, and opened doors for her within the company.

With the support of her mentor and the Women in Tech group, Alex could navigate challenges, develop her skills, and progress in her career. She became an active participant in the network, sharing her experiences, mentoring junior colleagues, and advocating for greater representation of women in leadership positions. Alex's journey exemplifies the transformative power of supportive networks and how they can create a thriving workplace environment.

TechConnect's success story shows companies can leverage supportive networks to foster an inclusive and thriving workplace. By providing resources, mentorship opportunities, and platforms for connection, organizations can empower employees to reach their full potential and contribute to the company's overall success.

Celebrating Your Achievements and Success

Acknowledging and celebrating our achievements is essential for maintaining motivation and a positive mindset. In our journey of self-improvement and growth, taking the time to recognize the progress we've made and the milestones we've reached is paramount to staying on track and continuing our upward trajectory.

Napoleon Hill, renowned author, and personal development pioneer, once wrote, 'Whatever the mind can conceive and believe, it can achieve.' Hill's timeless wisdom reinforces the importance of celebrating achievements as a powerful tool for manifesting our desires and aspirations.

When we take the time to acknowledge and celebrate our successes, we affirm our belief in our capabilities and fuel our determination to continue reaching new heights. By celebrating our achievements, we set a positive momentum in motion, attracting even more remarkable accomplishments into our lives. Let us remember Hill's timeless advice as we embrace the art of celebration on our personal and professional growth journey.

Another quote I love to live by is from an Unknown author: "Celebrate your small victories; they lead to bigger accomplishments."

This reminds me of the significance of celebrating small victories because they act as stepping stones toward achieving bigger accomplishments. Acknowledging and celebrating our small wins boosts our confidence, motivation, and well-being. It creates a positive feedback loop, where each small success reinforces our belief in our abilities, making us more likely to take on bigger challenges.

Celebrating small victories also helps us maintain momentum and focus on our goals. It provides a sense of progress and accomplishment, even when the overall journey may seem long or challenging. Recognizing and appreciating these small steps makes us more likely to persevere through obstacles and setbacks.

Ultimately, celebrating small victories is about fostering a growth mindset and cultivating a habit of recognizing progress and achievement, no matter how seemingly insignificant.

The Practice of Gratitude

Gratitude is a powerful and transformative force that can shift our perspective from focusing on what we lack to appreciating what we have. We develop a greater sense of contentment, happiness, and resilience by cultivating gratitude.

Practical Actions

Here are some practical strategies I advocate for:

- Maintaining a gratitude journal. This simple yet powerful exercise involves regularly jotting down what we are grateful for, including our achievements and progress. Reflecting on our accomplishments and expressing gratitude for them in writing can profoundly impact our overall well-being and attitude toward life. It helps us stay focused on the positive aspects of our journey and provides a gentle reminder of our progress.

- Organizing milestone celebrations is another way to commemorate achievements and boost team morale. Whether it's a personal milestone like completing a challenging project or a collective milestone like reaching a sales target, recognizing these moments in a meaningful way fosters a sense of unity and camaraderie within the team. Celebrations can take various forms, such as team lunches, themed parties, or special awards ceremonies.

- Engaging in personal reflection exercises is also instrumental in celebrating achievements. Taking time to reflect on the journey we've embarked on, the obstacles we've overcome, and the growth we've experienced allows us to internalize our successes. Through introspection, we gain a deeper understanding of our strengths, areas of improvement, and the resilience we've demonstrated along the way.

- Create meaningful rituals to honor our accomplishments, no matter how small they may seem. These rituals involve treating ourselves to something we enjoy, spending quality time with loved ones, or simply giving ourselves a moment of quiet appreciation for our efforts.

Celebrating achievements and successes is equally motivating in a team environment. When small victories are celebrated, we build a culture of positivity and growth within ourselves and our teams. It fosters a supportive environment where everyone feels valued and encouraged. It encourages collaboration and a sense of camaraderie as we cheer each other on and celebrate collective successes.

Research supports the idea that celebrating achievements has numerous benefits. According to studies conducted by Harvard Business School professor Teresa Amabile and psychologist Martin Seligman, recognizing and celebrating small wins enhances motivation, productivity, and overall job satisfaction. It creates a positive feedback loop that fuels our drive to accomplish more.

Practical actions for leaders:
Team building activities are a great way to celebrate success, express gratitude and reinforce a positive and cohesive work culture.

Here are some team-building activities that can be used to celebrate achievements and foster camaraderie among team members:

- Team Recognition Ceremony: Organize a formal team recognition ceremony to acknowledge and celebrate individual and team accomplishments. Provide certificates, plaques, or awards to recognize their contributions.
- Escape Room Challenge: Take the team for a fun and challenging escape room experience. This activity encourages teamwork, problem-solving, and communication skills while celebrating successes.
- Team Building Games: Plan team-building games that promote collaboration and friendly competition. Games like "Minute to Win It" or scavenger hunts can be enjoyable ways to celebrate while building team spirit.
- Outdoor Adventure: Arrange an outdoor adventure activity such as a hiking trip, camping, or team-building ropes course. These activities encourage teamwork, trust, and mutual support among team members.
- Team Lunch or Dinner: Treat the team to a special lunch or dinner at a nice restaurant. This allows everyone to relax, socialize, and celebrate in a more informal setting.
- Creative Workshop: Organize a creative workshop or art activity where team members can express themselves through painting, crafts, or other artistic pursuits. This fosters creativity and provides a unique way to celebrate success.

- Team-Building Retreat: Consider a team-building retreat where team members can engage in workshops, discussions, and team-building activities while enjoying some downtime and relaxation.
- Volunteer Together: Celebrate success by contributing to the community as a team. Choose a charitable project or organization to volunteer with and make a positive impact together.
- Office Games and Competitions: Plan friendly office games and competitions like a trivia challenge, ping pong tournament, or board game showdown. These activities promote friendly rivalry and celebration.
- "Show and Tell" Session: Encourage team members to share their successes and accomplishments in a "show and tell" session. This allows everyone to appreciate each other's contributions and celebrate achievements collectively.

Tailor the team-building activities based on the preferences and interests of your team members. The key is to create an atmosphere of celebration and appreciation while providing opportunities for team bonding and relationship-building. Celebrating success through team-building activities can boost morale, strengthen team dynamics, and contribute to a positive work environment.

Nurturing Mental, Spiritual and Physical Health

In Chapters 3 and 4, we have talked a lot about emotional health: understanding ourselves, expressing and managing emotions in a healthy and constructive manner, and being resilient, nurturing mental, spiritual, and physical health is crucial for empowerment as these complete the foundation for overall well-being and success in life. Just as emotional health shapes our inner world, these other aspects contribute to our overall equilibrium, empowering us to embrace a life of fulfillment and purpose.

Spiritual, Physical and Mental Health: Understanding the Vital Connection

Let's delve deeper into why nurturing these three dimensions of health is essential for empowerment:

Spiritual Health:

Spiritual health forms the foundation of our well-being, embracing purpose, connectedness, and inner peace. Nurtured through various practices—religion, nature, art, and introspection—it fosters resilience and inner guidance. Mindfulness, gratitude, and self-reflection in spiritual practices promote balance and harmony, enriching our lives with fulfillment and purpose.

Faith, intertwined with spiritual health, offers hope and trust beyond ourselves, providing strength and meaning to life's journey. Nurturing our spiritual well-being positively impacts our mental, emotional, and physical health, leading to a more profound sense of connection and peace within ourselves and others.

Physical Health
Our bodies are the vessels through which we navigate the world and pursue our goals. Maintaining good physical health is fundamental to empowerment as it enhances energy levels, focus, and productivity. Regular exercise, a balanced diet, and sufficient rest and sleep are essential to physical well-being. When we prioritize our physical health, we feel more capable of tackling challenges, taking on new opportunities, and embracing a vibrant and active lifestyle.

Mental Health
A strong and resilient mind is the cornerstone of empowerment. When we prioritize our mental health, we build the capacity to handle challenges, setbacks, and stressors more effectively. By cultivating a positive and

balanced mindset, we can overcome self-doubt, fears, and limiting beliefs that may hinder our progress. Taking care of our mental health through mindfulness, meditation, and self-reflection enables us to make clear decisions, set meaningful goals, and stay focused on our aspirations. Some of the tips were mentioned in the earlier sections of this book.

Statistics emphasize the significance of prioritizing mental and physical health. According to a study by the World Health Organization, depression, and anxiety disorders cost the global economy over $1 trillion annually in lost productivity.

On the other hand, organizations prioritizing employee well-being and providing resources for mental health support experience higher employee engagement, lower absenteeism, and improved overall performance.

The interconnectedness of mental, spiritual, and physical health is undeniable. When these dimensions are nurtured, and in balance, they create a harmonious foundation for personal growth and empowerment. Investing in our well-being enhances our self-esteem, confidence, and sense of agency.

Sense of agency refers to the belief and feeling that one has control over their actions and the ability to influence their own life and circumstances. The sense of being in charge of one's choices and decisions can lead to a greater sense of empowerment and self-efficacy. A strong sense of agency allows individuals to take the initiative, set goals, and actively pursue their aspirations, contributing to a more proactive and fulfilling life experience.

This means that when we invest in our well-being, such as taking care of our physical, spiritual, mental, and emotional health, we experience positive changes in ourselves. It boosts our self-esteem, which is our belief in our worth and abilities. Additionally, it increases our confidence, making us more assured in our decisions and actions. Moreover, nurturing our well-being gives us a greater sense of agency, the feeling that we have control over our lives and can influence outcomes. All of these combined contribute to a more empowered and fulfilled version of ourselves.

Empowerment is not just about achieving external success but also about building inner strength and resilience to navigate life's complexities with grace and determination.

When Courageous Conversation Was Not an Option

A person dear to me is known for their strong work ethic and determination. As an immigrant, they saw every opportunity as a chance to build a better life for themselves and their family. They poured their heart and soul into their job, striving to meet the high expectations set by both their employer and themselves.

However, as the demands at work grew, the person carried an increasingly heavy load. Their workload seemed never-ending, and they often had to take on tasks beyond their job description and lots of overtime due to staffing issues. Despite the mounting pressure, they remained dedicated and hopeful, believing their efforts would lead to better days.

This impactful situation exemplifies a courageous conversation that regrettably faltered in its attempt to be heard. Despite their heartfelt pleas for support and understanding from management, their voices fell on deaf ears. They bravely expressed their concerns about the poorly managed workload and the need for additional staff to alleviate the burden. Still, it seemed as if no one was listening. The lack of proper supervision and guidance only added to their frustration and feelings of being overwhelmed.

The relentless pressure took a toll on their mental health as time passed. Burnout started to creep in, leaving them feeling exhausted and drained. They pushed through, refusing to show any signs of weakness, but eventually, the toll became too much to bear. The once vibrant and enthusiastic person I knew started to withdraw, their energy fading and their smiles becoming scarce.

Their mental health began to deteriorate, leading to more serious issues affecting their well-being and relationships with family and loved ones. They struggled to balance work and personal life, and their family could see its toll on them.

Seeing someone I cared about suffering due to a work environment that seemed indifferent to their well-being was troubling and disheartening. It's a situation where courageous conversation was not an option, the issues remained unresolved, and the work environment was unsupportive. The management's neglect of their employees' concerns had severe consequences, not just for this person but for the entire team's morale and motivation.

This gut-wrenching experience taught me the importance of advocating for mental health and well-being in the workplace. No one should have to sacrifice their health and happiness for the sake of a job.

Finding the right balance between advocating for change and taking care of yourself is essential. If the work environment remains unsupportive despite your best efforts, it may be worth considering if the organization aligns with your values and long-term goals.

This is just one story that highlights the need for organizations to create a culture that prioritizes the well-being of their employees and listens to their concerns. I'm sure there are more stories like this out there.

How do I know?

Just look at the rates of absenteeism, employees on medical leave and staff turnover.

These statistics can speak volumes about the state of well-being and support within an organization. High rates of absenteeism, employees on medical leave, and staff turnover can be indicators of a toxic or unsupportive work environment. When employees struggle with burnout, stress, or mental health issues, their productivity and engagement are likely to suffer, negatively impacting the organization's overall success.

Leaders and decision-makers must recognize the correlation between employee well-being and organizational success. Investing in the well-being of employees is not just a gesture of goodwill; it is a strategic move that can yield significant benefits for the organization. A healthy and supportive work environment fosters higher employee engagement, job satisfaction, and commitment to the organization's goals.

Practical Actions
To address these challenges and create a culture that prioritizes employee well-being, I urge you to take the following steps:

- **Conduct well-being assessments**: Regularly assess employee well-being to identify potential issues and areas for improvement. Use surveys, focus groups, or anonymous feedback mechanisms to gather honest employee insights.
- **Actively manage and balance team's workload**: Work with employees to set achievable and realistic goals that consider their capacity and skill level. Avoid overwhelming them with unrealistic expectations that can lead to stress.
- **Implement support programs**: Offer a range of support programs, such as Employee

Assistance Programs (EAPs), mental health resources, and wellness initiatives. Encourage employees to take advantage of these resources without fear of stigma or reprisal.

- **Train managers and leaders**: Provide training to managers and leaders on how to recognize signs of burnout and stress in their team members. Equip them with the skills to have open and supportive conversations about well-being and work-life balance.
- **Create a flexible work environment:** Offer flexible work arrangements to accommodate employees' personal needs and responsibilities. This can help reduce stress and improve work-life integration.
- **Foster a culture of open communication:** Create a culture where employees feel comfortable voicing their concerns and providing feedback without fear of retaliation. Ensure that their voices are heard, and that action is taken to address their needs. Encourage regular check-ins to discuss progress and identify potential challenges.
- **Recognize and celebrate achievements**: Acknowledge and celebrate employees' accomplishments and contributions. Regular recognition can boost morale and motivate employees to continue giving their best.

This loved one's journey through burnout and mental health struggles serves as a reminder that we all have a responsibility to support and care for one another. By fostering a compassionate and empathetic work environment, we can help prevent burnout and empower each other to achieve success without sacrificing our mental health and personal lives.

As leaders, we hold the power to shape the work environment to create a space where each team member can flourish. It's our responsibility to prioritize the well-being of our teams and create a culture that values mental, spiritual, and physical health. Empowerment becomes a reality when we prioritize the well-being of our employees and actively address their needs.

Chapter 8
Writing Our Future

"Do not just create your future.
Create for yourself a BETTER future."
- Maria Drueco, 2019

In 2019, I was invited to speak at an event. As I took the stage that day, I was met with a sea of eager faces, each representing a unique story of resilience and determination. This event, hosted by one of the immigrant associations in the city, was an opportunity to connect with individuals who had embarked on journeys similar to mine - the journey of being an immigrant in a new land.

As I glanced across the eager faces in the audience, I could feel their anticipation and excitement to hear what I had to share. It was evident that they were there not only to listen but to seek inspiration and guidance. And at that moment, I knew the importance of my message—to empower them to create a better future, not to let themselves be boxed in, be stuck, to make better goals, and to unlock their true potential.

I knew everyone sitting before me had already shown incredible strength and courage by stepping into the unknown, leaving their comfort zones behind.

As I began to speak, I shared my personal story. I opened about the challenges I faced, the obstacles I overcame, and the moments of doubt I encountered along the way.

"Each of you has a unique story, a unique set of skills, and a unique contribution to make. Do not let anyone or anything define your worth or limit your potential. Embrace your differences, for they are your strengths. Seek opportunities, take risks, and never stop learning."

The room was filled with nods of understanding and smiles of encouragement. Their eyes reflected the resilience they had gained through their unique experiences.

I shared stories of immigrants who had come before us, who had overcome adversity and achieved remarkable feats. These stories were not just about finding a job or building a career; they were about individuals who had carved their path to greatness, positively impacting their communities and beyond.

"In life, it's not enough to simply go with the flow and let circumstances dictate our future," I continued. *"Instead, we have the power to*

design our destiny. Do not just create your future. Create for yourself a BETTER future."

"When you 'just create' your future," I explained, *"you may be taking a passive approach, simply accepting whatever unfolds without actively shaping it. It's like drifting along a river, letting the currents carry you wherever possible. While this approach might lead you somewhere, it may not necessarily be where you truly want to be."*

"In contrast," I continued, *"when you aim to 'create a better future,' you are purposefully designing and working towards a vision that surpasses the status quo. It means setting clear goals, envisioning your desired life, and taking intentional steps to get there. It's like steering a ship towards a destination, knowing that each move you make brings you closer to your dreams. We are not passive participants in our destinies but active creators of our own narratives."*

Drawing upon personal experiences and stories of resilience, I emphasized the importance of setting ambitious goals, dreaming big, and daring to imagine a future that surpassed their current circumstances. I encouraged them to speak up when the situation necessitates, embrace challenges as catalysts for growth, seeing obstacles as stepping stones to success rather than barriers to their dreams. I emphasized that creating a better future requires a mindset of continuous progress and a determination to elevate one's life and circumstances. It was about seeking growth, improvement, and positive change in every aspect of their lives.

As the event ended, I felt a sense of satisfaction knowing that my words resonated with the attendees. I had planted a seed of empowerment to fuel their determination to build a brighter future for themselves and their loved ones.

To this day, I am still in touch with some of those individuals, following their progress and celebrating their achievements.

This experience reinforced my belief in the transformative power of intentionality and the importance of empowering others to unleash their potential. It reaffirmed the core message of this book: that by harnessing the power within ourselves and setting our sights on a better future, we can create a life filled with purpose, fulfillment, and lasting impact.

Setting Goals and Taking Action

As an avid traveler, my heart always longed for the mystique and wonders of far-off lands. Egypt, with its rich history and ancient marvels, had been at the top of my bucket list for as long as I could remember.

My wanderlust led me to the land of pharaohs and mysteries this time. And there was also a more profound yearning within me—to walk in the footsteps of history, to visit the places mentioned in the Bible. Tracing the path where the Holy Family once sought refuge in Egypt filled me with a profound sense of connection to the ancient past.

I embarked on this transformative journey with careful planning and excitement brewing in my heart. Exploring the bustling streets of Cairo, I imagine the traders and travelers of antiquity making their way through the same vibrant marketplaces. Every historical site I visited— Karnak, Luxor, and the Valley of the Kings— brought the stories of ancient Egypt to life before my very eyes.

Yet, the prospect of visiting places that held significance in biblical narratives genuinely touched my soul. Arriving at the site where the Holy Family was believed to have found refuge during their sojourn in Egypt, I felt an indescribable connection with my faith.

Standing there, I pondered the story of the Holy Family's life as exiles in Egypt, and the sacred moments that had taken place where I stood.

The climb to Mount Sinai's top was another endeavor with spiritual and historical implications. Our group started climbing at midnight. As I ascended, I reflected on the countless pilgrims and travelers who had undertaken this same journey, seeking solace and divine guidance. Watching the sunrise from the summit, I couldn't help but feel a profound sense of reverence, knowing that I was witnessing a sight that had inspired countless hearts throughout history.

Careful planning and preparation were essential for a seamless experience throughout my adventure. I had set my sights on Egypt's historical wonders and places of spiritual significance, and each step I took brought me closer to fulfilling my dreams. Embracing every moment, whether planned or unforeseen, I discovered the beauty of the unexpected, the magic of human connection, and the awe-inspiring history permeating Egypt's very essence.

During the trip, our group encountered a series of unexpected delays caused by numerous checkpoints that dotted the landscape. The delays were an unforeseen challenge that threatened to disrupt our meticulously planned itinerary.

At first, frustration and impatience tried to take root within me. But I knew that moments like these were inherent in travel. Embracing the spirit of adventure, I took a deep breath and found a sense of calm amidst the waiting.
Rather than letting the delays dampen my spirits, I used this unexpected pause to engage with fellow travelers, discovering their stories and experiences and learning about the places they had visited. I exchanged tips and recommendations, immersing myself in the collective knowledge of my fellow explorers, which enriched my own adventure.

As we eventually got to the last checkpoint, I emerged with a renewed sense of patience and an appreciation for the journey. I realized that while delays might have shifted my schedule, they hadn't diminished the grandeur of Egypt's wonders or the transformative nature of my travels. With a re-adjusted schedule, I delved even deeper into the historical riches of Egypt.

S.U.C.C.E.S.S Framework
A Holistic Approach to Goal setting and Achievement

What's the point of my Egypt story? In life, just like in any travel to a destination, the pursuit of our aspirations and achieving our goals, be it personal, professional, or business, follow a similar path of setting clear objectives, taking purposeful action, embracing the journey, and finding fulfillment.

However, the path to accomplishing our aspirations is often filled with challenges, uncertainties, and the need for adaptability.

To navigate this intricate journey effectively, use the **S.U.C.C.E.S.S Framework** (Figure 7) — a holistic and versatile approach to goal setting and achievement. A roadmap designed to empower and inspire.

The **S.U.C.C.E.S.S Framework** embodies the belief that success goes beyond reaching the destination. It emphasizes the journey's significance, where every step, setback, and triumph contributes to our growth and fulfillment. Rooted in the principles of clarity, commitment, resilience, and collaboration, this framework offers a comprehensive guide to those striving to achieve their dreams.

S.U.C.C.E.S.S. Framework

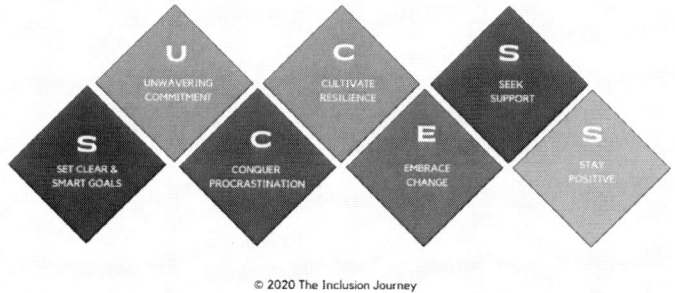

Figure 7: **S.U.C.C.E.S.S. Framework**

At the core of the S.U.C.C.E.S.S Framework lies the word "SUCCESS" itself, each letter representing an essential element in the process of setting and pursuing goals:

S - Set Clear and SMART Goals

The first step in the S.U.C.C.E.S.S Framework is to set clear and SMART goals. Define what you want to achieve with clarity and precision.

- SMART is an acronym for Specific, Measurable, Achievable, Relevant, and Time-bound. Use these criteria to make your goals more effective.
- Ensure that your goals are specific and well-defined, measurable to track progress, achievable within your capabilities, relevant to your overall vision, and time-bound with a clear deadline.

U - Unwavering Commitment

- Embrace unwavering commitment to your goals. Make a firm decision to pursue them wholeheartedly.
- Develop a detailed plan of action for each goal.
- Consider any potential obstacles or challenges that may arise and develop contingency plans to overcome them.
- Stay focused on your objectives, and let your passion drive your actions.

C - Conquer Procrastination and Take Action

Procrastination can hinder progress. Conquer this challenge by taking consistent action toward your goals to achieve success. Every small step you take brings you closer to realizing your aspirations.

- Break your goals down into smaller, actionable steps. Identify the specific tasks or milestones you need to achieve along the way. Breaking goals into smaller parts makes them more manageable and helps you stay focused.
- Regularly monitor and track your progress towards your goals. This allows you to assess your performance, adjust as needed, and stay motivated. Use tools like progress trackers, checklists, or habit trackers to help you stay accountable.

C - Cultivate Resilience in the Face of Challenges

- Challenges are inevitable on the path to success.
- Embrace them as catalysts for growth.
- Cultivate resilience.
- View setbacks as opportunities to learn, adapt, and become stronger.

E - Embrace Change and Adaptability

- Be open to change and adaptability. Embrace the twists and turns that come your way. Sometimes, your original plan may need adjustments.
- Stay flexible while keeping your vision in mind.

S - Seek Support and Collaboration

Success is not a solitary journey.

- Seek support from mentors, friends, or colleagues.
- Collaboration can bring fresh perspectives and collective wisdom to help you achieve your goals.

S - Stay Positive and Mindful

- Maintain a positive mindset.
- Cultivate gratitude and practice mindfulness.

- Staying positive helps you navigate challenges with optimism, and mindfulness keeps you anchored in the present moment.
- Celebrate your achievements along the way. Each milestone reached is an opportunity to acknowledge your progress and motivate yourself to keep going. Start celebrating small wins to boosts your confidence and reinforce your commitment to your goals.

The **S.U.C.C.E.S.S Framework** is not a one-size-fits-all formula; instead, it offers a dynamic and adaptable approach tailored to our needs and circumstances. It empowers us to embrace our unique paths, encouraging personal growth and inspiring others.

In our journey towards personal and professional development, the **S.U.C.C.E.S.S Framework** is an invaluable guide - our compass. This compass leads us toward our goals while instilling in us the wisdom to cherish the process, embody success, and inspire others to embark on their own transformative journeys.

Ultimately, the true essence of setting goals and taking action lies in finding fulfillment in the pursuit itself. Celebrating the small victories, cherishing the moments of connection with others, and discovering the hidden gems of life's journey is all part of the rewarding tapestry of living with purpose and intention.

Conclusion
Embrace Your Journey,
Empower Your Future

Congratulations on completing this transformative journey with **"UnHide Yourself™: Break Free from Bias, Stigma, and Stereotypes,** *Empower Yourself, Empower Your Team."*

Together, we've explored a rich tapestry of insights, practical strategies, and empowering stories that illuminate the path to personal and collective empowerment.

Chapters 1 & 2 of the book unveiled the impact of bias, discrimination, and microaggressions on underrepresented groups. It emphasizes the power of sharing our stories and the importance of cultivating self-confidence, embracing our unique identities, and nurturing self-worth and belief in our abilities.

Chapter 3 guided us through the power of sharing our stories and the significance of embracing our unique identities, cultivating self-confidence, and unleashing our true potential.

In Chapter 4, we delve deep into cultivating self-confidence. We explore techniques to nurture our self-worth and belief in our abilities and how to build confidence, self-awareness, and personal empowerment. We also learn how to harness our unique strengths and turn challenges into opportunities, empowering us to navigate life's hurdles with resilience and determination.

In Chapter 5, we embraced courageous conversations, armed with the **UnHide Yourself Blueprint,** to champion diversity, equity, and inclusion in our workplaces. We addressed bias in hiring, confronted microaggressions, and became advocates for transformative systemic change. We understand why this blueprint matters and its impact on individuals, leadership, teams, and organizations. The 9 Steps to **UnHide Yourself™** guide us through phases that help us embrace transformative change, from confronting biased hiring and promotion practices to responding to microaggressions and stereotypes.

In Chapter 6, we tackle the complexities of addressing discrimination in the workplace, amplifying our voices, and advocating for systemic change. We equip ourselves with the **R.E.S.P.E.C.T. Conversation Tool,** empowering us to navigate difficult situations, and advocate for fairness and inclusivity.

The essence of well-being took center stage in Chapter 7, where we explored strategies for resilience, financial empowerment, and the beauty of building supportive networks through mentorship and allyship. I shared the **Empowered A.L.L.Y.S. Framework** as a guide on how to be an effective ally. Throughout our journey, we celebrated our achievements. We understood the profound importance of nurturing mental, spiritual, and physical health, ensuring a balanced and harmonious existence.

Finally, in Chapter 8, we took the pen into our hands, embracing the **S.U.C.C.E.S.S Framework,** setting ambitious goals, and taking purposeful action to create a better future for ourselves and our teams.

As you conclude this book, remember that empowerment knows no boundaries. You hold the key to unlocking your true potential and igniting change around you. **"UnHide Yourself™"** is not just a book; it's a movement.

Thank you for joining me on this empowering adventure. Together, we are breaking barriers, embracing diversity, and creating a world where each voice matters. Remember, you are an unstoppable force, and your journey toward personal and collective empowerment has just begun.

Let's continue to **UnHide** ourselves and illuminate the path for others, leaving an enduring legacy of inclusivity and progress.

The power to transform is within you. Embrace it. Empower yourself. Empower your team.

Next Steps

Now that you've reached the end of **"UnHide Yourself™: Break Free from Bias, Stigma, and Stereotypes (Empower Yourself, Empower Your Team),"** it's time to put your newfound knowledge and inspiration into action.

Here are some next steps to consider:

1. **Reflect and Internalize**: Reflect on the insights and lessons you've gained from the book. Internalize the key messages and how they resonate with your experiences and aspirations.
2. **Set Personal Goals:** Utilize the **S.U.C.C.E.S.S Framework** outlined in Chapter 8 to set clear and ambitious personal goals. Define specific Practical Actions that align with your vision for a better future.
3. **Advocate for Change**: Armed with the **UnHide Yourself™ Blueprint** from Chapter 5, be a catalyst for change within your workplace and community. Advocate for diversity, equity, and inclusion, and initiate courageous conversations to address bias and discrimination.
4. **Build a Supportive Network:** Chapter 7 explored the importance of building a supportive network. Reach out to mentors, join Employee Resource Groups (ERGs), and become an ally to others in your journey toward empowerment.

5. **Celebrate Achievements:** Don't forget to celebrate your achievements, big or small. Acknowledge your progress and take time to appreciate your growth along the way.

6. **Prioritize Well-being:** Embrace self-care strategies outlined in Chapter 7 to nurture your resilience and overall well-being. Remember that taking care of yourself is essential in sustaining your empowerment journey.

7. **Stay Curious and Keep Learning:** This journey doesn't have to end here. Continue seeking knowledge, exploring new perspectives, and staying curious about different cultures, experiences, and ideas.

8. **Share Your Story:** As we learned in Chapter 3, the power of our stories can inspire and empower others. Consider sharing your experiences and insights with your community or through platforms where your voice can make a difference.

9. **Empower Others:** Pay it forward by empowering others. Become a mentor or advocate for someone who needs support and guidance.

10. **Invest in your groups or organization's continuing education:** Receive discounts on bulk purchases of **UnHide Yourself™: Break Free from Bias, Stigma, and Stereotypes (Empower Yourself, Empower Your Team).** To order in bulk, mail us at maria@theinclusionjourney.com

Remember, this is not just the end of a book; it's the beginning of your empowered journey. Embrace your uniqueness, seize growth opportunities, and let your light shine as you create a better future for yourself and those around you. You have the power to make a lasting impact. Go forth, unhide yourself, and be the change you wish to see.

Let's Work Together: Empower Yourself, Break Free from Bias, and Drive Positive Change

Working with me is an opportunity to embark on an empowering journey towards unmasking your true potential and that of your team, and breaking free from the limitations imposed by bias, stigma, and stereotypes.

Here's how we can collaborate:

1. **Speaking Engagements**: Invite me to speak at your events, conferences, or seminars to inspire and empower your audience. I'll ignite the spark of transformation within your community through impactful storytelling and

actionable insights. You can reach me by email: maria@theinclusionjourney.com

2. **Inclusive Talent Solutions (Comprehensive DEI & Talent Management Consultation Service):** Organizations seeking to build a more inclusive and supportive workplace can benefit from my expertise in creating strategies focused on DEI in talent-related matters to create an inclusive and engaged workforce. I provide audit and consultation services to help you implement effective and sustainable initiatives that foster an empowered and diverse workforce.

3. **Workshops and Training:** I offer interactive workshops and training sessions for organizations, teams, and individuals seeking to foster diversity, equity, and inclusion. These sessions focus on developing a deeper understanding of unconscious bias, microaggressions, anti-racism, inclusive leadership, inclusive teams, intercultural communications, and creating courageous conversations to drive positive change.

4. **Coaching Sessions:** Through one-on-one coaching sessions, we'll delve deep into your experiences, aspirations, and challenges. Together, we'll identify areas where you seek growth and empowerment. I'll provide tailored guidance, strategies, and support to help you overcome obstacles and achieve your goals.

5. **Online Resources:** Stay connected with my empowering content through online platforms.

Engage with my blog, social media, and educational resources. I share valuable insights and practical tools to support your empowerment journey.

6. **UnHide Yourself™ Community**: Join a community of like-minded individuals passionate about driving positive change and creating a world where everyone can thrive. Participate in group discussions, share your experiences, and connect with others on similar journeys.

Together, we'll navigate the complexities of bias, stigma, and stereotypes, empowering you to embrace your unique identity, amplify your voice, and drive transformational change in your personal and professional life. I'm committed to supporting you every step of the way as you unhide yourself and embrace a future filled with purpose, fulfillment, and empowerment. Let's unlock your potential and make an impact together!

Maria Nathalia Drueco

Website: www.theinclusionjourney.com

About the Author

 Maria Drueco is a highly skilled Talent Management Consultant, Equity, Inclusion, and Diversity Strategist, Anti-Racism Educator, and Intercultural Trainer/Facilitator with over a decade of experience in the Human Resources industry. Her professional journey has involved working with medium to large-sized organizations, including the pharmaceutical, healthcare, tech, travel industries, and the public sector, where she has provided invaluable guidance and coaching to leaders at all levels, from executives to front-line supervisors.

With a specialized focus on equity, inclusion, diversity, anti-racism work, and equitable talent management, Maria brings a wealth of expertise to her role. What sets her apart is her personal experiences as an immigrant in Canada and as a member of an underrepresented group, which have granted her a profound understanding of the impact of microaggressions, stereotypes, workplace bullying, and discrimination.

Maria's commitment to creating and advancing inclusion, equity, and anti-racism work shines through her various online and in-person workshops, training sessions, facilitation, and keynote speeches. Her passion is to help leaders cultivate a diverse workforce and foster an equitable, inclusive, healthy, and resilient organizational culture. She has extensive experience as a presenter, both locally and internationally. She is adept at delivering engaging content both online and in-person.

In addition to her professional endeavors, Maria is a passionate entrepreneur and owns and operates a travel business that focuses on enriching people's spiritual and cultural experiences. This endeavor allows her to combine her love for travel and exploration with her dedication to promoting intercultural understanding and appreciation.

Beyond her professional and entrepreneurial pursuits, Maria actively supports non-profit organizations and dedicates her time mentoring new immigrants through the Edmonton Region Immigrant Employment Council (ERIEC). She is also a volunteer Board Member for International Personnel Management Association – Canada (IPMA-Canada), a long-standing non-profit HR organization in Canada dedicated to promoting HR excellence.

With her unwavering dedication to supporting her community, Maria strives to make a positive impact by empowering organizations to embrace diversity, foster inclusivity, and create thriving and resilient workplaces while enriching individuals' spiritual and cultural experiences through her travel business.

To book Maria as a speaker or to learn more about her services, please visit www.theinclusionjourney.com, or contact her directly at maria@theinclusionjourney.com

Follow Maria on social media to stay updated on her latest speaking engagements, articles, and insights:

- LinkedIn: www.linkedin.com/in/maria-nathalia-drueco-talentmgmnt-edistrategist-speaker
- Twitter: @DruecoMaria

Notes

Chapter 1

Sala, Marbella A. and Dankwa-Mullan, Irene. "Understanding and Addressing Racial Bias in Medicine" .The New England Journal of Medicine, 2021.

Eberhardt, Jennifer L. "Biased: Uncovering the Hidden Prejudice That Shapes What We See, Think, and Do". Viking, 2019.

Harvard Implicit Bias Test by Project Implicit - A collection of online tests and research on implicit biases: https://implicit.harvard.edu/

Corrigan et al , Patrick W. "The Stigma of Mental Illness: Effects of Labeling on Public Attitudes" . Health and Social Behavior, 2003.

Goffman, Erving. "Stigma: Notes on the Management of Spoiled Identity". Simon & Schuster, 1986.

Organization: World Health Organization (WHO) - "Reducing stigma and discrimination" section: https://www.who.int/mental_health/policy/stigma/en/

Devine, Pauline G. "From Prejudice to Discrimination: The Steps of Stereotyping". Journal of Personality and Social Psychology, 1989.

Steele, Claude M."Whistling Vivaldi: How Stereotypes Affect Us and What We Can Do". W. W. Norton & Company, 2010.

UNESCO - "Fighting against stereotypes, prejudices, and discrimination" section: https://en.unesco.org/themes/fighting-against-stereotypes-prejudices-and-discrimination

Kamalu , N.N.and Kamalu, N.N. "The Intersectionality of Race, Gender, and Immigration Status: Implications for Social Service Delivery".Journal of Sociology and Social Welfare, 2019. Available at: https://scholarworks.wmich.edu/jssw/vol46/iss1/9/

Sweet, E., and Miner, K. "The Unique Stigmas Faced by Immigrant Women" Center for American Progress, 2018. Available at: https://www.americanprogress.org/issues/women/reports/2018/07/19/453884/unique-stigmas-faced-immigrant-women/

Frieze, I., Roos, P., & Kaur, T. "The Double Jeopardy of Being an Immigrant Woman: The Interplay of Gender and Ethnicity in Discrimination" 2008.

Clance, R.S., & O'Yoole, G.L."Imposter Syndrome and Minority Students: A Multicultural Approach to Counseling College Students" Journal of College Student Development, 1988.

Chait Barnett, R.M. and Hirschhorn, L."Tokenism in Employment Contexts: The Historical and Psychological Implications of Tokenism" Human Relations, 1993.

Bertrand, M & Mullainathan."Diversity and Inclusion in Organizations: Conceptualizing Cultural Fit and the Effects of Stereotype Threat on Affirmative Action Hiring Practices" American Economic Review, 2004.

Chapter 2:

Statistics Canada: "Mental Health of Canada's Immigrant and Refugee Children: Segmented Assimilation, Ethnic Density Effects, and Demographic and Socioeconomic Context." Available at: https://www150.statcan.gc.ca/n1/pub/89-599-m/89-599-m2005006-eng.htm

Centre for Addiction and Mental Health (CAMH): "Racialization and Health Inequities in Toronto." Available at: https://www.camh.ca/-/media/files/pdfs---camh-racialization-and-health-inequities-in-toronto-pdf.pdf

Catalyst: "Women of Color in the United States." Available at: https://www.catalyst.org/research/women-of-color-in-the-united-states/

Conference Board of Canada: "Indigenous Women in Leadership: From Classroom to Boardroom." Available at: https://www.conferenceboard.ca/e-library/abstract.aspx?did=10113

Canadian Centre for Diversity and Inclusion (CCDI): "Unconscious Bias and Microaggressions in the Workplace." Available at: https://ccdi.ca/unconscious-bias-and-microaggressions-in-the-workplace/

Sue, D. W., Capodilupo, C. M., Torino, G. C., Bucceri, J. M., Holder, A. M. B., Nadal, K. L., & Esquilin, M. (2007). "Racial microaggressions in everyday life: Implications for clinical practice." American Psychologist, 62(4), 271-286.

Torino, G. C., & Fricker, M. (2016). "Microaggressions and moral cultures." Journal of Social Philosophy, 47(1), 72-91. Richards, D. A. R., & Hackett, R. D. (2012). "Cultural diversity and teamwork in healthcare: A scoping review of the literature." BMC Health Services Research, 12, 1-17.

Purdie-Vaughns, V., & Eibach, R. P. (2008). "Intersectional invisibility: The distinctive advantages and disadvantages of multiple subordinate-group identities." Sex Roles, 59(5-6), 377-391.

Ely, R. J., & Thomas, D. A. (2001). "Cultural diversity at work: The effects of diversity perspectives on work group processes and outcomes." Administrative Science Quarterly, 46(2), 229-273.

King, E. B., Dawson, J. F., West, M. A., Gilrane, V. L., & Peddie, C. I. (2017). "Why organizational and community diversity matter: Psychological safety and innovation." Journal of Applied Psychology, 102(11), 1683-1698.

Brown, B. (2012). Daring Greatly: How the Courage to Be Vulnerable Transforms the Way We Live, Love, Parent, and Lead. Avery

Harvard Business Review. (2019). Diversity and Inclusion: The Reality Gap. Retrieved from https://hbr.org/2019/07/diversity-and-inclusion-the-reality-gap

McKinsey & Company. (2020). Diversity Wins: How Inclusion Matters. Retrieved from https://www.mckinsey.com/business-functions/organization/our-insights/diversity-wins-how-inclusion-matters

Neff, K. D., & Germer, C. K. (2013). A Pilot Study and Randomized Controlled Trial of the Mindful Self-Compassion Program. Journal of Clinical Psychology, 69(1), 28-44.

Eagly, A. H., & Karau, S. J. (2002). Role congruity theory of prejudice toward female leaders. Psychological Review, 109(3), 573-598

Dasgupta, N., & Asgari, S. (2004). Seeing is believing: Exposure to counterstereotypic women leaders and its effect on the malleability of automatic gender stereotyping. Journal of Experimental Social Psychology, 40(5), 642-658

Hebl, M. R., & Mannix, L. M. (2003). The weight of obesity in evaluating others: A mere proximity effect. Personality and Social Psychology Bulletin, 29(1), 28-38.

Chapter 3
Bravata, D. M., et al. (2019). Association between self-reported beliefs and objectives and quality improvement outcomes: a cross-sectional study. Journal of General Internal Medicine, 34(1), 49-56.

Dweck, C. S. (2006). Mindset: The New Psychology of Success. Random House.

Neff, K. (2011). Self-Compassion: Stop Beating Yourself Up and Leave Insecurity Behind. William Morrow Paperbacks.

Roberson, Q. M., & Kulik, C. T. (207). Stereotype threat at work. Academy of Management Perspectives, 21(2), 24-40.

Smith, L. G., et al. (2019). The Relationship between Ethnic Identity, Self-Esteem, and Job Satisfaction in a Sample of Latina Nurses. Hispanic Health Care International, 17(4), 175-181.

Chapter 4
Cohen, S. (2004). Social relationships and health. American Psychologist, 59(8), 676-684.

Gucciardi, D. F., et al. (2017). Mental toughness in sport: Motivational antecedents and associations with performance and psychological health. Journal of Sports Sciences, 35(24), 2425-2434.

Hülsheger, U. R., et al. (2019). Mindfulness as a moderator of the relation between work engagement and burnout: A two-sample study. Journal of Organizational Behavior, 40(2), 166-183.

Luthar, S. S., et al. (2000). Developmental psychopathology: Perspectives on adjustment, risk, and disorder. Cambridge University Press.

Avery, D. R., McKay, P. F., & Volpone, S. D. (2007). Group diversity and performance: The moderating effects of diversity belief. Group & Organization Management, 32(5), 590-607.

Bravata, D. M., Watts, S. A., Keefer, A. L., Madhusudhan, D. K., Taylor, K. T., Clark, D. M., & Lin, N. D. (2019). Prevalence, predictors, and treatment of impostor syndrome: a systematic review. Journal of General Internal Medicine, 34(3), 508-518.

Dweck, C. S. (2006). Mindset: The new psychology of success. Random House.

Hülsheger, U. R., Alberts, H. J., Feinholdt, A., & Lang, J. W. (2013). Benefits of mindfulness at work: The role of mindfulness in emotion regulation, emotional exhaustion, and job satisfaction. Journal of Applied Psychology, 98(2), 310-325.

Judge, T. A., & Hurst, C. (2007). Capitalizing on one's advantages: Role of core self-evaluations. Journal of Applied Psychology, 92(4), 1212-1227.

Neff, K. D. (2011). Self-compassion: Stop beating yourself up and leave insecurity behind. HarperCollins.

Roberson, Q. M., & Kulik, C. T. (2007). Stereotype threat at work. Academy of Management Perspectives, 21(2), 24-40.

Smith, L. L., Renkema, L. J., Martin, C. R., & Vardaman, J. M. (2019). Exploring identity integration as a mediator of work–life balance's relation to job satisfaction and organizational commitment. Journal of Business and Psychology, 34(6), 801-818.

Chapter 6
Gino & Staats. "Why Organizations Don't Learn. (2015) https://hbr.org/2015/11/why-organizations-dont-learn

Gino, F., & Wilmuth, C. (2015). The Bias Against Creativity: Why People Desire But Reject Creative Ideas. Harvard Business Review.

Hunt, V., Layton, D., & Prince, S. (2018). Why Diversity Matters. McKinsey & Company.

Center for Talent Innovation. (2013). Innovation, Diversity, and Market Growth

Karsai, I., & Beier, M. E. (2016). Introduction: Sexism and discrimination in the workplace.

Karsai & M. E. Beier (Eds.), Sexism and Stereotypes in Modern Society: The Gender Science of Janet Taylor Spence (pp. 215-222). Taylor & Francis.

Williams, J. C., & Dempsey, R. (2014). What Works for Women at Work: Four Patterns Working Women Need to Know. NYU Press. https://www.businessinsider.com/every-company-that-was-sued-discrimination-and-harassment-lawsuits-2020-2021-1

Pager, D., Western, B., & Bonikowski, B. (2009). Discrimination in a Low-Wage Labor Market: A Field Experiment. American Sociological Review, 74(5), 777-799.

Dobbin, F., & Kalev, A. (2016). Why Diversity Programs Fail. Harvard Business Review, 94(7/8), 52-60.

Greenwald, A. G., Banaji, M. R., & Nosek, B. A. (2015). Statistically Small Effects of the Implicit Association Test

Can Have Societally Large Effects. Journal of Personality and Social Psychology, 108(4), 553-561.

Pager, D., & Shepherd, H. (2008). The Sociology of Discrimination: Racial Discrimination in Employment, Housing, Credit, and Consumer Markets. Annual Review of Sociology, 34, 181-209.

Pager, D. (2007). The Use of Field Experiments for Studies of Employment Discrimination: Contributions, Critiques, and Directions for the Future. The Annals of the American Academy of Political and Social Science, 609(1), 104-133.

Chapter 7

Kabat-Zinn, J. (2013). Full catastrophe living: Using the wisdom of your body and mind to face stress, pain, and illness. Bantam.

House, J. S., Landis, K. R., & Umberson, D. (1988). Social relationships and health. Science, 241(4865), 540-545.

Lyubomirsky, S., King, L., & Diener, E. (2005). The benefits of frequent positive affect: Does happiness lead to success? Psychological Bulletin, 131(6), 803-855.

Ham, S., & Kim, J. (2009). Travel as a learning experience: A phenomenological study. Tourism Management, 30(3), 408-418.

Sood, A. (2016). The Mayo Clinic Guide to Stress-Free Living. Da Capo Lifelong Books

Hanh, T. N. (1999). The Miracle of Mindfulness: An Introduction to the Practice of Meditation. Beacon Press. Kabat-Zinn, J. (2005). Wherever You Go, There You Are: Mindfulness Meditation in Everyday Life. Hachette Books.

Neff, K. D. (2011). Self-compassion: The proven power of being kind to yourself. HarperCollins.

National Association of School Psychologists. (2020). Helping children after a crisis. Retrieved from https://www.nasponline.org/resources-and-publications/resources-and-podcasts/school-climate-safety-and-crisis/mental-health-resources/helping-children-after-a-crisis-tips-for-parents-and-teachers

Case, K. A., & Hunter, C. D. (2012). All Allies Aren't Created Equal: The Impact of White Gatekeeping on Social Justice Activism. Journal of Social Issues, 68(1), 78-92.

Downing, N. E. (2008). The White Privilege Role in Social Justice Education: Deconstructing White Privilege to Promote Social Justice Activism. Multicultural Perspectives, 10(4), 205-210.

Kandasamy, N., Chua, R. Y. J., & Ingram, P. (2019). From Opponent to Ally: Signaling Value Change Through

Interpersonal Influence. Organization Science, 30(6), 1196-1217.

Neville, H. A., Spanierman, L. B., & Doan, B. T. (2006). Exploring the Association between Color-Blind Racial Attitudes and Latina/o College Students' Perceptions of Campus Climate and Other Outcomes. Journal of Diversity in Higher Education, 9(3), 135-154.

Singh, A. A., & Harrison, K. M. (2016). Building Bridges or Walking the Talk? Examining Allyship and Advocacy among Asian American and Pacific Islander LGBTQ Activists. American Journal of Community Psychology, 57(3-4), 345-357.

Ragins, B. R., & Cotton, J. L. (1999). Mentor functions and outcomes: A comparison of men and women in formal and informal mentoring relationships. Journal of Applied Psychology, 84(4), 529-550.

Allen, T. D., Poteet, M. L., & Burroughs, S. M. (1997). The mentor's perspective: A qualitative inquiry and future research agenda. Journal of Vocational Behavior, 51(1), 70-89.

Fagenson, E. A. (1989). When the mentor is a woman and the protege is a man: The significance of gender in the mentoring process. Journal of Organizational Behavior, 10(1), 39-53.

Williams, M. (2018). Google's Employee Resource Groups: Cultivating Diversity and Inclusion.

Microsoft. (n.d.). Employee Resource Groups at Microsoft. Amabile, T. M., & Kramer, S. J. (2011). The progress principle: Using small wins to ignite joy, engagement, and creativity at work. Harvard Business Review Press.

Seligman, M. E., Steen, T. A., Park, N., & Peterson, C. (2005). Positive psychology progress: Empirical validation of interventions. American Psychologist, 60(5), 410-421.

Chapter 8
Covey, S. R. (2004). The 7 Habits of Highly Effective People. Simon & Schuster.

Dweck, C. S. (2006). Mindset: The New Psychology of Success. Random House.

Grant, A. M. (2013). Give and Take: A Revolutionary Approach to Success. Penguin Books.

Manufactured by Amazon.ca
Acheson, AB

33513187R00171